Costing And Pricing In The Digital Age:

A PRACTICAL GUIDE FOR INFORMATION SERVICES
BY HERBERT SNYDER AND ELIZABETH DAVENPORT

The complexity of costing and charging for electronic information systems and services present a whole new financial challenge to librarians and other information service managers. This first guide to common accounting practices for these systems incorporates models, worksheets, sample scenarios, and exercises to illustrate methods for:

- identifying and understanding both fixed and variable costs associated with information technologies
- looking at the life cost of systems
- pooling and allocating costs across different financial organizations
- calculating the net present value of future payments
- setting prices for charge-backs and user fees involved with systems and services
- identifying and understanding the costs and issues involved in making the transition from print to electronic information sources
- developing internal auditing techniques and increasing financial controls for electronic services

Information specialists in all kinds of agencies can turn to this practical managerial and cost accounting resource to more effectively oversee, project, and forecast the significant costs associated with investments in information technology.

1-55570-311-9. 1997. 6 x 9. 175 pp. $45.00.

Creating A Financial Plan:

A HOW-TO-DO-IT MANUAL FOR LIBRARIANS
BY BETTY J. TUROCK AND ANDREA PEDOLSKY

Creating A Financial Plan shows librarians how to offset tight funding and rising costs by allocating (and accounting for) funds most effectively. Covered are matching financial resources to priorities; applying productivity and cost-finding techniques; setting and implementing financial goals and objectives; and creating a financial plan. Also included are helpful forms and worksheets and a basic glossary of financial terms.

1-55570-039-X. 1992. 8 1/2 x 11. 190 pp. $45.00.

"Highly recommended for new managers, directors of public libraries and all library managers unfamiliar with financial planning or needing an exact action plan." *Library Journal*

"The book is well organized, the style straightforward, and the advice, practical and informed by experience." *Canadian Law Libraries*

Financing Public Library Buildings

BY RICHARD B. HALL

Financial difficulties are a common plague of library facility projects — large or small. *Financing Public Library Buildings* is the first comprehensive treatment of this critical subject. Hall brings nearly twenty years of experience overseeing LSCA-funded building projects in two states to this detailed guide. All aspects of the process and realities of finding financial support are covered: planning library construction projects; project cost estimates; identifying and assessing potential funding sources; obtaining federal, state, and local government funding; and finding private funding. A summary ties everything together, and helpful charts, graphs, and worksheets (such as a method to figure average cost-per-square foot and a planning form for estimating construction costs) are provided throughout.

1-55570-165-5. 1994. 7 x 10. 299 pp. $65.00.

"...Hall's work is right on target. It is going to become one of the most-read books of its genre. For all professional collections." *Library Journal*

"Anyone...building a new library or undertaking another big library construction project should look at this...Highly recommended." *Booklist*

"...provides library managers, trustees, Friends of the library, and government officials with the information they need." *American Libraries*

Winning Library Referenda Campaigns:

A HOW-TO-DO-IT MANUAL
BY RICHARD B. HALL

Written by an expert consultant, here is an indispensable resource for any library trying to win community support. The manual opens with a nationwide analysis of capital referenda results during the last eight years. Other chapters cover establishing realistic goals by evaluating past referenda; the role of politics; campaign organization and calendar; market research and polling; targeting and timing campaign strategy; fiscal concerns and budgeting; legal issues; campaign volunteers; and handling the media. Numerous illustrations of bumper stickers, brochures, posters, and handouts actually used in campaigns are included.

1-55570-224-4. 1995. 8 1/2 x 11. 248 pp. $49.95.

"If you ever plan on having a funding referendum for your library, don't start without this book...will do everything for your campaign but vote. Buy it." *Library Journal*

"To make sure your referendum is successful, read *Winning Library Referenda Campaigns.*" *American Libraries*

"...explains everything planners and implementers need to know...from making the first commitment to the final vote." *Reference & Research Libraries News*

"A very useful book which will be of assistance to any public library. Recommended." *The Bottom Line*

NS

Neal-Schuman Publishers
100 Varick Street, New York NY 10013
212-925-8650   fax toll free — 800-584-2414
Website: http://www.neal-schuman.com

ISBN 1-55570-288-0

90000>

9 781555 702885

BUDGETING

A How-To-Do-It Manual for Librarians

Alice Sizer Warner

**HOW-TO-DO-IT MANUALS
FOR LIBRARIANS**

NUMBER 79

NEAL-SCHUMAN PUBLISHERS, INC.
New York, London

Published by Neal-Schuman Publishers, Inc.
100 Varick Street
New York, NY 10013

Printed and bound in the United States of America.

Library of Congress Cataloging-in-Publication Data

Warner, Alice Sizer.
    Budgeting : a how-to-do-it manual for librarians / by Alice Sizer Warner.
        p.   cm.—(How-to-do-it manuals for libraries ; no. 79)
    Includes bibliographical references (p.   ) and index.
    ISBN 1–55570–288–0
    1. Library finance—United States. I. Title. II. Series.
Z683.2.U6W37   1998
025.1'1—dc21   97–35960
                                                            CIP

CONTENTS

ACKNOWLEDGMENTS

This book was written in two locations: at our home in Lexington, Massachusetts, and in a pickup truck camper at Southwest Harbor, Mount Desert Island, Maine. Many people helped, a few are listed here.

Charles Harmon, Neal-Schuman editor, read and vetted this book many, many times.

As the book was first being put together, Anne Farlow Morris helped immeasurably with the section on getting grants.

As the book was nearing completion, Barbara Whyte Felicetti made excellent suggestions about sections that needed strengthening.

Students in my various classes helped more than they can possibly know.

And, of course, Caleb Warner did most.

Thank you all.

PREFACE

Budgeting: A How-To-Do-It Manual for Librarians is designed for librarians who are in some way involved with money: using money, asking for money, protecting the money they have, stretching money, doing without money, handling money, keeping track of money, planning for money, and, perhaps most happily, spending unexpected money.

Most of us—myself included—were not taught much about money in library school. I absorbed just two dicta: first, you can never, financially, afford to open a branch library, and second, you can never, politically, afford to close one—and that is literally all I remember from library school on the subject of money.

Some years after I got my library degree, I was lucky enough to undertake two activities: teaching a for-credit class on "fiscal management" at my alma mater, Simmons Graduate School of Library and Information Science in Boston, and developing a one-day continuing education course on budgeting for the Special Libraries Association.

One lesson that I had thoroughly learned at Simmons, from a delightful and skilled professor, was: "Always teach something you don't know—that way you'll always be learning something new." So I set out to learn about money and libraries and librarians. I read everything I could find, and, frankly, most of what I read was both excruciatingly abstruse and exquisitely boring. Reading the teaching materials that had been used by the professor who had taught the fiscal management course before me, I didn't (and still don't) understand what was given me. So I began taking people out to lunch, people who had great track records as library managers, and I asked for advice and picked their brains. I was determined that any class I taught was going to be interesting, useful, and lively. What you will read in this book is both a continuation and an expansion of what I learned then and keep learning now.

The Special Libraries Association budgeting course attracted 100 students the first time it was offered. This showed how much a money class was needed but was difficult as I had to lecture all day to this large group rather than have the luxury of setting up small group discussions. Eventually SLA and I settled on a version of the class that we called "Mainstreaming the Library"; it was, and is, about maneuvering things so a library is utterly essential to whomever holds its purse strings.

SLA also asked me several years ago to write a self-study program for them; I did, and emphasized the fact that special librarians have to "own" their numbers. The following anecdote demonstrates why that is so important:

A Student's Tale
One of my former students took, as a first job, the directorship of a tiny New England library. The furniture was terrible, patrons were getting splinters. My student, up in arms, went to the town's treasurer and demanded new tables and chairs. She left that office cowed, ashamed. She'd been unaware of the whole picture. She had not known her numbers. What the town really needed to spend its money on, she now saw, was a new fire engine: library furniture was low on the town's list. The treasurer gave her a handful of sand paper to use on her furniture and said he would be down on Saturday to help.

The tale's big lesson (aside from demonstrating the importance of knowing your numbers), of course, is that every library does things a little differently. Much of this book is based on examining the budgets acquired by Simmons students, as well as by students at the University of Michigan and the University of North Carolina at Chapel Hill—schools where I also have been privileged to teach. (The first homework assignment for students in my classes is to go out and find a budget, any budget, that has to do with a library or an "information something": these budgets are used for class study.) *Budgeting: A How-To-Do-It Manual for Librarians* represents what all these students and I have together learned. Our approach may be unorthodox, yet the hope is that this volume will be helpful to readers as a first book, a primer, an introduction to money and the libraries that money serves.

Chapter 1, "Numbers, Your Library, and You," is about the importance of being comfortable with numbers, of knowing one's numbers, of owning one's numbers. Anyone who handles a library's budget must feel comfortable talking about numbers.

Chapter 2, "Kinds of Budgets," speaks about six popular manners of budgeting: lump sum, formula, line-item, program, performance, and zero-based budgeting (known "affectionately" as ZBB). Many library budgets are, and should be, expressed in more than one of these manners, and we should know how to do this.

Chapter 3, "Measuring Ourselves," addresses issues to do with finding out where, quantitatively, our libraries stand among peers. Most libraries are covered by some sort of formal standard, and certainly we should know by what standard we are measured and how we measure against that standard. Almost more useful than formal standards, though, are generally held perceptions, rule-of-thumb standards, many of which are detailed in chapter 3. These rules of thumb can perhaps be called common knowledge—impossible to document or to prove, yet acutely useful as measuring tools. Chapter 3 also discusses keeping statistics about one's library, and about how to use those statistics when talking with management; remember: management is used to dealing in numbers, and statistics are numbers.

Chapters 4 and 5 examine using resources outside the immediate scope of a library's budget. Chapter 4, "Alternate Resources: Grants and Endowments," deals with money coming to the library from outside sources. Three sources of grant money are explored: from corporations, from foundations, and from "the government." Grant money is to be spent when received, usually for a particular purpose. Endowment money, however, is invested, and only the income from endowment investments is spent. The chapter explores many forms, from jewelry to stock shares, in which endowment money may come.

Chapter 5, "More Alternate Resources: Volunteers, Fund Raising," covers volunteer programs in libraries. Truly effective volunteer programs do not simply happen; they are made to happen. Using volunteers in a library is not simply a matter of saving money; satisfied volunteers are good public relations—volunteers are voters, and voters are those who support a library. Chapter 5 also includes ideas about how library volunteers can raise extra money for a library—from book sales to "murder parties."

Chapter 6, "Fees for Library Services," talks about charging back, charging out, and/or charging fees. Charging back involves no visible funds; charge backs are debits, are internal, paper charges against the individual or the department that uses library services. Charging out happens when a client comes to a firm (e.g., an accounting or legal firm) for service; if the library participates in service to the client, the client is billed appropriately for the library's services. Charging fees happens when an outside client comes to a library, requests service, gets it, and then pays for it; fee-based services happen in public libraries, academic libraries, and increasingly in special libraries. Chapter 6 also suggests how a fee-based service in a library can market itself, and closes with brief reference to how a library might learn from, and use, independent librarians.

Chapter 7, "Living with the Budget," touches on ongoing budget issues: keeping track of the budget as time goes on, planning the budget, budget hints for a librarian in a new job, hints for the budget and a new library, the budget and a new building, and suggestions as to how a librarian might present a budget. The last section in chapter 7 looks at managing a library's budget when budget cuts loom.

Each chapter in this book is followed by a section called "Questions to Help You Focus." No reader, of course, is expected to do all of the exercises, but you may wish at least to read them over. And some readers may find that actually doing some of the exercises may help to turn their thinking toward real budget know-how, toward comfort with numbers.

Many librarians have a "Who, *me?*" knee-jerk reaction to dealing with money, with budgets. Many of us are still giggling over a cartoon (whose origin is lost, I'm afraid) where the king is sitting on his throne, watching an energetic court jester twirl and juggle and dance. The king's question: "Sayyy...do you know anything about budgets!" *Budgeting: A How-To-Do-It Manual for Librarians* is designed to empower, to help readers to understand their budgets, to put these budgets into larger contexts, to deal intelligently with their budgets, actually to own their budgets. My hope is to help readers eradicate this "knee-jerk reaction."

I believe it was Nathaniel Hawthorne who said, "An easy read is a damned hard write." Writing this book has been, of course, hard. I hope the reading of it will not be.

Good luck!

1 NUMBERS, YOUR LIBRARY, AND YOU

This chapter is about learning how to be comfortable around, to talk about, to use, and to understand your library's "numbers," and how to ask for explanations when you don't understand the numbers. In addition to knowing our own library's numbers, we should also know about the numbers for other, comparable libraries.

Learn how to dare to try to think about numbers, to think in numbers. Learn how to talk about numbers, to understand numbers, to ask other people about their numbers. Know the language of numbers. Get used to dealing with "ballpark figures."

"FACTOIDS"

The American Library Association puts out a wallet-sized leaflet that contains "quotable facts about America's libraries."[1] Virtually all of these "factoids" involve numbers. Some of these may be useful when you talk with others about your library's budget.

Regarding the U.S. government: "Federal spending on libraries totals only 57 cents per person—about the cost of a pack of gum." "In 25 years, federal funding for libraries comes to less than the cost of one aircraft carrier (est. $3.5 billion)."

About academic libraries: "College librarians answer 94 million reference questions each year—more than three times the attendance at college football games." "College and university libraries loan 180 million items each year at a cost of $1 billion. If students and faculty had to purchase these materials, they would have to pay $8 billion!"

School libraries: "Americans spend nine times as much on home video games ($1.5 billion) as they do on school library materials for their children." Compare this to: "Students visit school library media centers some 1.7 billion times during the school year—about twice the number of visits to state and national parks."

And public libraries: "Americans check out an average of six books a year and spend an average of $18.73 a year in taxes for public library service—the same as one hardcover book." "Americans spend $330 billion a year on legalized gambling—enough to fund public libraries for the next 75 years."

My favorite example of how a library made its point by using numbers occurred more than two decades ago. The Massena, NY,

Public Library published a mailable broadside entitled "This Is How We Did It," the "It" being how that library provided well over $1.3 million of service with a budget of just under $116,000. They started with the biggest amount, "You borrowed 157,235 regular books—buying them at our price ($8.32) you could have spent $1,308,195.20." They moved on to, "Seamstresses borrowed 520 patterns and saved $780.00," and ended up with, "We held a puppet workshop for 8 children, $80."[2]

More recently, the Orville, Ohio, Public Library claimed that citizens "saved" $4,016,686—this figure being computed as the value of items checked out minus the library's budget of $469,552. Among these items: 4,037 books on tape (at $70 each); 5,954 music audiocassettes (at $15 each); 5,979 compact disks ($15 each); 34,844 videocassettes ($20 each).[3]

Libraries here in Massachusetts have made similar statements.[4] The Framingham Public Library "proved" (they even published the facsimile of a check made out to "the Townspeople of Framingham") that their $1.2 million budget gave a 738 percent return on investment—that their services were worth $9.1 million: "11,500 of you visited area museums . . . by borrowing our passes; full admission would have cost you at least $11,750." The Hudson Public Library did much the same, claiming their $287,929 budget gave over $2.9 million of service (130,092 books checked out, at an average cost $20 per book, would have cost a reader $2,601,840). My own hometown (Lexington) insisted that their $1 million budget gave $31 million worth of services.

When others discuss their numbers, ask for explanation when you do not understand, ask for help in relating the numbers you hear to numbers you do understand. Ask questions. Do not be hesitant about saying, "Help me put this in perspective, could you?" Learn how to estimate. Be comfortable with rounding numbers. Learn how to talk easily about figures and dollars.

USING SPREADSHEETS TO TALK ABOUT NUMBERS

An amazingly large number of librarians are unacquainted with computer spreadsheet programs.[5] Most librarians know about the automated facilities in use in their libraries and are facile when it comes to using word processing; increasing numbers of librarians are using e-mail daily. But spreadsheet knowledge is not common, and it must so become. If you do not have a spreadsheet conveniently available and installed, remedy the situation immediately. Spreadsheets are not difficult to learn to use, and there are many varieties available.

Using a word processer makes writing words infinitely quicker, easier, and more accurate than using a typewriter or a pen. Similarly, using a spreadsheet makes dealing with numbers infinitely quicker and easier and more accurate than using a ledger pad, a pencil with a large eraser, and a calculator. Possible spreadsheet uses are virtually limitless.

It helps to think of a spreadsheet as a huge sheet of ledger paper, of cross-patch (graph) paper. Horizontal lines create rows, vertical lines create columns, and the intersections of the lines create what are called cells. Each cell has an easily understood "address" made up of numbers and letters. And spreadsheets, like word processors, allow the user to be human—to insert, to erase, to change, to rearrange.

Data entered into a spreadsheet can be a constant value that does not change—a date, for instance, or a number on last year's budget, or the name of a person or of a budget line. Or data entered into a spreadsheet can be treated as a variable—next year's budget figures, for instance, which the spreadsheet permits us to vary via simple arithmetic or via formula.

Use of a spreadsheet encourages use of "what if?" scenarios. Were library employees to get a 4 percent cost-of-living increase, what would this do to the budget? If next year's library book sale were to bring in $6,000 and not the usual $10,000, what would this do to the budget?

Use spreadsheets as a tool to help understand numbers, to help talk about numbers.

SIMILAR LIBRARIES

Know the figures for libraries similar to your library, so you can keep your own library's numbers in perspective. And share what you learn with other libraries (possibly via listservs). Ask yourself the following questions: (1) What is the total budget of your library? (2) What is the total budget of the organization that your library serves? (3) What percent of the organization's budget goes to your library? (4) How does this compare to similar libraries that serve other organizations?

For instance, if your library is a public library, what percentage of your municipality's budget goes to your library? How does this compare to library budgets in other nearby towns with approximately the same population as your town? How do other towns' budgets compare to your town's?

If your library is an academic or school library, how does your library's budget compare to those of similar academic institutions? What percentage of your academic institution's budget goes to the library? Compare your school library budget to library budgets of similar-sized schools in similar-sized areas.

Special librarians may find it a bit more difficult to get details about other special libraries' budgets, as special libraries often are found in for-profit, and therefore competitive, businesses; why, argue some, should one for-profit business tell a competitor details about how the business (including the library) is run? And yet any information that can be found can be helpful.[6]

TALKING ABOUT MONEY

Once you've embarked on efforts to learn about numbers, to talk about numbers, to deal in numbers, the task of understanding those numbers becomes infinitely easier. Many of us were taught as children that it is not nice to talk about money, and this remains true in most social situations. And yet library management is not a social situation, it is a business situation. Responsible librarians must talk about money, they must deal in numbers. As Kimberly Taylor, director of the Colorado Center for the Book, has said, "Money is a neutral object. Nonetheless, it elicits emotional reactions because of the charge each person places on it."[7] When discussing numbers, when talking about money, we librarians must learn to be objective and unemotional.

QUESTIONS TO HELP YOU FOCUS

FACTOIDS

A. What "factoids"—quotable facts—might be developed using your library as source material?
B. What is spent per year, per user?
C. What does this amount of money compare to?
D. How many reference questions are answered per year?
E. How many items are loaned to users each year? What would these items cost if directly purchased by the users?
F. Can you think of other questions that might lead to authoritative-sounding factoids?

SPREADSHEETS

A. What kind of computer are you using for word processing?
B. Is there a spreadsheet program on this computer?
C. If so, what is the name of the spreadsheet program?
D. If not, what is the name of the proposed spreadsheet program?
E. Using directions that come with the spreadsheet program, set up a simple spreadsheet. Suggestion: use the example found in chapter 7, "Living with the Budget": The Simmonsville Public Library. Using the spreadsheet, try the suggested scenarios—awarding raises, spending money on the furnace, etc.

SIMILAR LIBRARIES, TALKING ABOUT MONEY

A. What is the total budget of your library? Ask. Talk with the director, the controller, the treasurer, the managing director, with whomever can give this information.
B. What is the total budget of the organization that your library serves? Find out. Ask.
C. What percent of the organization's budget goes to your library? Figure this out.
D. What are the above figures for libraries similar to yours? Ask. Talk with other librarians in those libraries.
E. How do your own library's figures compare to those of similar libraries? Make these comparisons. Talk with others at your library about these comparisons. Talk with those at other libraries.

NOTES

1. All of the following factoids are from a wallet-sized leaflet of factoids available from American Library Association (ALA), 50 E. Huron St., Chicago, IL 60611, tel. 800–545–2433.
2. "This Is How We Did It" was reprinted in *The U*N*A*B*A*S*H*E*D Librarian* 19 (March 1976): 3.
3. The Orville, Ohio, Public Library data was cited in *Library Administrator's Digest* (April 1995): 31.
4. Massachusetts libraries' information was taken from ads and fliers distributed by the towns involved.
5. Two useful sources about using library spreadsheets are: Marilyn E. Barnes, "Quick and Clean: A Fast Path to Library Spreadsheet Systems," *The Bottom Line* 8:1 (Summer 1994): 38–49; and Lawrence W.S. Auld, *Computer Spreadsheets for Library Applications*, 2d ed. (Phoenix, AZ: Oryx, 1993).
6. Chapter 3 of this book discusses rule-of-thumb budget standards for various kinds of libraries.
7. Kimberly Taylor, "Getting to Yes: A Fundraising Attitude That Works," *The Bottom Line* 5:4 (Winter 1991–1992): 33.

Another helpful article for budgeting beginners is Carol Pitts Diedrichs, "Off to See the Wizard—Demystifying Your Financial Relationships," *Library Administration and Management* 10:2 (Spring 1996): 105–109.

The publisher of the book you are reading offers many books related to fundraising, financial planning, and management. Their catalog is available from Neal-Schuman Publishers, Inc., 100 Varick St., New York, NY 10013.

2 KINDS OF BUDGETS

This chapter discusses six types of budgets, all of which are employed at one time or another by most kinds of libraries. Which budget type to use, and when, depends both on requirements of the institution the library serves, and on the application for which the library's budget will be used.

There are as many variations of budgets in use as there are libraries in existence.[1] Most library budgets fall into one of the following six broad categories:

1. lump sum
2. formula
3. line item (also called line)
4. program
5. performance (also called function)
6. zero-based

LUMP-SUM BUDGETS

In lump-sum budgeting, the librarian is given an amount of money with which to run the library, much as our foremothers were given sums of money to run their households: one takes what is given and does what one can.

The problem for the librarian (as well as for our grandmother) is that a lump-sum budget dictates the library's services and programs. Its real weakness is that little or no prior consideration has been given to what the library's services and programs ought to be so that these services and programs themselves can help define the dollars available to carry them out. A librarian dealing with a lump-sum budget may have difficulty relating that budget both to the goals of the library and to the goals of the larger organization the library serves.

A librarian faced with a lump-sum budget needs to resolve many questions. For instance, does the librarian have free rein in dividing up the lump sum, or are there rules to follow? If, in planning the budget, decisions are made, may these decisions be reversed or changed as the year goes on? How will the librarian's progress be monitored? What kinds of budget reporting are expected of the librarians?

Fortunately, we see little supersimplistic lump-sum budgeting in today's library world. There might be the occasional situation where a librarian is given a windfall, along with vague instructions: "Here's what we've got, see how far you can go with a bookmobile program" (or service for seniors, or a library branch at the dockyard, whatever).

My mother, as part of her volunteer "war work" during World War II, took on the task of allotting $1,000 (a substantial amount in those days) from the state for materials for our tiny New England public library—a task for which she'd had no training whatsoever. "Shakespeare," she asked, "or mysteries?" She received no guidance at all, so she did the best she could and determined what the library's resources should be: for high schoolers, a one-volume complete works of Shakespeare (beautifully illustrated, as I remember, by Rockwell Kent); for our farm families, lots of materials on growing chickens and canning vegetables and using root cellars; and for everyone a gorgeous pile of new children's books and as much adult "escape reading" as she could afford.

FORMULA BUDGETS

Formula budgeting is also often used in government, as well as in universities. A formula budget allows each part of a government body or academic institution to be measured equally and compared equitably. Formula budgeting involves allocating money according to, literally, a formula that usually is based on numbers of people. Community colleges, for instance, have library materials budgets that follow a formula that takes into account the number of FTE ("full-time equivalent") registered students. Those libraries do not know exact budget amounts until registration closes, usually well into the second week of each term.

Most formula budgets in libraries determine which materials are purchased for which areas of study. At many universities, library materials budgets are allocated according to the percent of student enrollment in each discipline; so, if 41 percent of students are enrolled in nursing studies, 41 percent of the library's materials budget goes for nursing.[2]

Most of us remember getting gold stars for perfect elementary school attendance. Being rewarded for showing up each day certainly said something about scholastic enthusiasm, about robust health, and about our parents' efficiency in sweeping us out the door. Most of us are unaware, however, that schools are reimbursed by some states based on a formula derived from the number of students who actually, physically show up each day. Schools are not reimbursed merely for how many students are enrolled: the more days kids show up, the more money the school gets from the state.

LINE-ITEM BUDGETS

A line-item budget (also known as a line budget, or, occasionally, "an incremental budget") is the most common library budgeting method. Each category of expenditure and income is represented by a line. Common lines or categories can be personnel, print, media, and so forth.

In many organizations, each budget line has an identifying number to help standardize budgets from department to department within the organization. For instance, if personnel costs are assigned the number category "600" in every budget in town, a town treasurer's life will be simpler.

Line-item budgets are easy to prepare. Below is a bare-bones example:

Line-Item Budget

Personnel	_____
Print	_____
Media	_____
Miscellaneous	_____
TOTAL	_____

Sometimes it is useful to indicate what percentage of the total each line encumbers.

Line-Item Budget (with percentages)

	Amount	Percent
Personnel	_____	_____
Print	_____	_____
Media	_____	_____
And so forth	_____	_____
Miscellaneous	_____	_____
TOTAL	_____	100%

It can be helpful to compare what was spent last year, line by line, to what is projected to be spent this year, line by line. In preparing the line budget for what we plan to spend next year, many simply adjust each line by a certain percentage.

Line-Item Budget

	Last year	Current year	±% Change	Projected next year
Personnel	_____	_____	_____	_____
Print	_____	_____	_____	_____
Media	_____	_____	_____	_____
And so forth	_____	_____	_____	_____
Miscellaneous	_____	_____	_____	_____
TOTAL	_____	_____	_____	_____

Line-item budget problems do carry some limitations, including a tendency to perpetuate "once a line, always a line," past mistakes. In addition, new lines are added as new needs and their costs creep in and need lines of their own. Comparing last year to this year to next year is never as easy or as static as one would like to believe.

As with formula budgets, a line budget is difficult to relate to the goals of the library and of the organization the library serves.

Each institution has its own categories for its line budget. Some standard income lines are:

- Appropriations
- Endowment income
- Fees and charges
- Fines
- Friends of the Library
- Gifts
- Interest
- Memberships
- Various grants

Common expenditure line-items are:

- Audiovisual
- Binding
- Books
- Computers (hardware, supplies, maintenance)
- Conference fees
- Consortium fees
- Consultants
- Database expense
- Duplication
- Fund drive expenses
- Equipment and furniture

- Microforms and related equipment
- Personnel, i.e., salaries and benefits (also called "personnel services")
- Rent
- Royalties
- Service contracts
- Software licenses
- Staff training
- Supplies
- Travel (often allotted among in-state, out-of-state, and foreign)
- Utilities

Since there is no one "right" way to "set up" a budget, many budgets have somewhat uniquely named lines. These lines obviously suit the library in question, and yet outsiders might not even know what the line means. Examples of individualistic income lines actually in use in today's libraries are:

- Columbus anniversary celebration
- Conscience money for overdue books
- Improvement through State Aid
- Insurance bond
- Late income from last year's Antique Show
- Unidentified contribution of $1,000

And here are some unusual expenditure categories:

- Anticipated 03 Tailings—approx 10%
- Browsery
- Burglar alarms
- Carpet repair
- Casual students
- Mass printing
- Microproducts
- Rags and wax
- Razing buildings
- Return freight charges
- Room fans
- Single Business Tax
- Tennis court lights
- Water treatment chemicals

PROGRAM BUDGETS

In program budgeting, service is the focus: a program budget shows what the library does for the people it serves and highlights what library users receive.

The first time an active, functioning library undergoes program budgeting is never easy for those who set up the initial pilot program budget. They need to determine, for example, what exactly are the library's programs. Some programs are obvious (such as the bookmobile, teenage activities, reference services); others are hidden (such as the special library that functions as "purchasing agent" for employees' desk-copy subscriptions, dictionaries—i.e., working materials).

Once programs are identified, it is important to find out how library staffers spend time, program by program. A careful survey of how each person's time is allocated during a "typical" week can uncover embarrassments: people easily become defensive when pushed to specify how they spend their time. However, a program budget exercise can uncover a remarkable amount of useful information.

Some public libraries exist in towns that use program budgeting for the whole municipal budget. One such library might come under a town program called Cultural Services. The library's subprograms could include Administration and Support, Central Library Services, Branch Library Services, Children's Services, Circulation and Support Services, and Plant Maintenance. Within each of these subprograms would be other programs, broken down to levels useful for their managers. One public library in a small New England town has: Administration, Community Service, Circulation, Collection Development, Reference, Children's Library, Technical Services, Custodial, and Sundays/Overtime.[3] Programs in a special library might include: Access to online materials, Alerting service, Telephone reference service, Filing service, and so forth.

A program budget might look like this:

Program Budget

	Administr. Services	Public Services	Technical Services	TOTAL
Personnel	___	___	___	___
Print	___	___	___	___
Media	___	___	___	___
And so forth	___	___	___	___
Miscellaneous	___	___	___	___
TOTALS	___	___	___	___
%	___	___	___	100%

Program budgeting is a crucial tool in measuring library programs and library activity against the goals of the organization the library serves. Quantitative questions can be considered: "We're spending three times as much on Program #2 as we are on #3—is #2 three times more important to our goals than #3 is? Should we shift a bit, perhaps divide things and introduce new categories #4 and #5?"

When presenting a budget to powers that be, that budget is almost always a line-item budget. Budget reviewers tend to look at big numbers, big lines, and try to cut them down. But let's say your library's telephone budget is challenged; one way to respond is to whip out the appropriate program budget and say, "Here are the programs we all agreed on; from which program do you suggest telephone support be removed?"[4]

PERFORMANCE BUDGETS

A performance budget (also known as a function budget) is similar in structure to a program budget. Instead of highlighting library programs, however, performance budgets concentrate on what library staff does. A performance budget parallels the line-item budget: lines from the line-item budget are broken down according to staff functions, much as programs are divided in the program budget above.

In a public library, functions might include: technical services (such as processing materials, cataloging, making collection available); circulation services (such as checking out and receiving materials, collecting overdue fines, shelving); reference services (everything from fielding telephone queries to showing patrons how to use computers, answering questions, chasing interlibrary loans); and planning (including budget management, trustee work, studying automation options, keeping up network relationships, interviewing potential employees).

A performance budget might look like this:

Performance Budget for the Technical Services Department

	Ordering Books	Cataloging Books	Processing Books	TOTALS
Personnel	___	___	___	___
Print	___	___	___	___
Media	___	___	___	___
And so forth	___	___	___	___
Miscellaneous	___	___	___	___
TOTALS	___	___	___	___
%	___	___	___	100%

One advantage of this kind of budget is that per-unit costs can be isolated. The classic example involves cataloging books: if one of the functions is to catalog books, and 100 books are cataloged for $100, then the library can associate a unit cost of $1 for each book cataloged. Another advantage of a performance budget is that the library director can plan for and monitor what staff members do and what it costs.

Performance budgets can be useful management tools. The danger, of course, is that quantity, not quality, of activity is measured. And what is measured does not directly reflect the goals of the library and of the organization it serves.

ZERO-BASED BUDGETS

Zero-based budgets (ZBBs) are extremely closely linked to the goals of the library and the organization the library serves.[5]

Zero-based budgeting focuses on the future. Unlike other forms of budgeting, ZBB is not based on what happened last year, nor is it based on what is happening now; last year's budget is not even considered. The future, and what is to be accomplished in this future, is paramount.

A zero-based budgeter (much like a program budgeter) concentrates on the services the library will provide during the coming year. A zero-based budget (ZBB) identifies what activities the library should make happen during the year, and projects costs for each activity. (In ZBB-language, an activity is called a "decision package.") Goals and their benefits are defined and strategies are outlined for achieving them. There is careful analysis of priorities; there is active thinking about discarding services, adding services, doing things differently. Eventually, decision packages are agreed upon.

For each decision package, a "decision package statement" is prepared, usually in a specific, predetermined format. Decision package statements answer questions such as:[6]

1. What is the name of the program this statement describes (sometimes called "decision unit name")?
2. What is the purpose of the program (i.e., "objective of decision unit")?
3. Which steps are required to carry out the program?
4. Who will benefit from the program results, and how?
5. Are there alternatives to the program (i.e., Are there other ways to accomplish the objective, and why aren't we using them?)?
6. What are the consequences of no program?
7. What is the budget for the program?
8. What is the program's priority rank compared to other proposed programs?

After the above questions have been formulated and priorities decided upon, results are expressed in the form of a program budget: each program on this ZBB program budget is a decision package survivor.[7] (See Figure 2.1 for a sample decision package.)

Zero-based budgeting takes a lot of work. In the library world, ZBB is used primarily by a new director when taking on a large and complicated library system as a way to get to know a very great deal about the library system, the people in it, the challenges being both faced and fended off, and the relationship of activity to goals. For a new director, a ZBB exercise gives a thorough introduction and indoctrination. If that director stays long enough, ZBB may well be repeated in five years, or seven, or ten.

ZBB has many advantages. Last year's budget is not taken as a base, goals are defined (often for the first time), money goes toward commonly agreed-upon goals, while less important activities are discarded.

There are ZBB disadvantages, primarily the fact that people (i.e., virtually all of us) are naturally threatened by change; it is all very well to think about new ways of getting things done as long as "*I* don't have to change." A very real ZBB disadvantage is that the process takes much time and much work in the midst

---

Figure 2.1. Zero-Based Budget: Sample Decision-Package Form

Program Name: _____   Rank: _____

Prepared by: _____   Date: _____

Description, Objective(s), and Goal(s): _____

_____

_____

Feasibility: _____

Requirements (personnel, supplies, etc.): _____

_____

Benefits: _____

_____

Activity as Currently Performed: _____

_____

Alternative Methods to Achieve Goal(s)/Objective(s): _____

_____

Budget: _____

Consequence(s) of <u>NOT</u> Approving This Package: _____

_____

****

Approved by: _____   Date: _____

of day-to-day library work. A more subtle disadvantage is that ZBB focuses on one year at a time, and many facets of libraries (such as some journals subscriptions) and institutions (such as long-term research projects) cannot be defined within the stricture of a year.

WHICH KIND OF BUDGET SHOULD YOUR LIBRARY USE?

There is no one right type of budget for every library in every year. Most ways of budgeting are useful, none serve perfectly, all are fallible.

When considering kinds of budgets, it is interesting to track how one line on one budget can become a lump-sum budget for someone else. For example, when a town meeting votes a budget for a library, the library is a line on the town's budget. Once the money gets to the library, that money is a lump, ready to be divided into lines again. At the library, perhaps there is a panel of teenagers who "advise" on how a few hundred dollars is to be spent on books for other teenagers: those dollars are a line on the library budget, yet the dollars are a lump sum for the teenagers, and they will argue to the penny how that lump sum should be spent.

As informed library managers, we need to keep at least a passing acquaintance with the various types of budgets, and to keep up with the numbers that surround our libraries, ourselves, and our communities.[8]

QUESTIONS TO HELP YOU FOCUS

LUMP-SUM BUDGETS
   A. Can you think of a specific library that uses a lump-sum budget?
   B. If you, as a librarian, were given a lump-sum budget to manage for a year, what questions would you have to ask of those who gave you the lump sum?

FORMULA BUDGETS

A. Can you think of a specific library with a formula budget?
B. How is the formula arrived at? Ask.
C. Do you feel the formula to be fair, equitable, ample, unfair, skimpy? Why? How does this formula compare to those in use at other, similar libraries?

LINE-ITEM BUDGETS

A. Examine the line-item budget for your own library.
B. Do you understand the lines as written? If not, ask.
C. Are the lines as written appropriate to the library, or primarily appropriate to the organization the library serves? What do you think about this?
D. Looking at the lines in your line-item budget, figure what percentage of the total is encumbered by each line. (If you do not remember how to figure out these percentages, ask someone to remind you how to do it. Do not be embarrassed to ask.)
E. Taking these percentages, rearrange the lines in the line-item budget so the biggest percentage appears at the top and the smallest at the bottom. What does this tell you?

PROGRAM BUDGETS

A. If your library has a program budget, what are the programs? How is the budget set up? Do you agree with what the programs are? Do you understand how the budget is set up?
B. If your library does not have a program budget, try to make one. How many programs will there be? How will the lines in the line-item budget be divided among these programs? (Note that program budgets are not easy to do; the first, the fifth, and possibly the tenth version will need redoing. Persevere.)
C. Analyze the program budget. What are the goals of your library? Do these programs address these goals? What other questions occur to you?

PERFORMANCE BUDGETS

A. If your library has a performance budget, what are the functions named in the budget? Do you agree with what these functions are? Do you understand how the budget is set up?
B. If your library does not have a performance budget, try to make one. How many functions will there be? How will

the lines in the line-item budget be divided among these functions? (Note that performance budgets are not easy to do; as for program budgets, persevere.)

ZERO-BASED BUDGETS

A. Has a zero-based budget been developed for your library, either now or in the past? If so, what do you think about the budget? What do you think about the choice of decision packages?

B. If your library has not developed a zero-based budget, try doing one yourself. Consult suggested readings on zero-based budgets, and remember that first experiences with ZBBs are always difficult.

C. Review the program budget you developed above. Do you still feel that the programs you specified are appropriate? Do you feel these programs should become decision packages for a zero-based budget (ZBB)?

D. Review the eight questions that might be asked when preparing a decision package statement.

E. Decide on the format for your ZBB—will there be a form to fill in for each decision statement, how long should/may each decision statement be, etc.?

F. Analyze the ZBB. Do the decision packages address the goals of the library? What do you feel about the budget as determined by the ZBB? What other questions occur to you?

WHICH KIND OF BUDGET TO USE?

A. Of the budgets developed above, which do you feel is most appropriate for your library?

NOTES

1. For more on defining kinds of budgets, see Robert D. Stueart and Barbara B. Moran, *Library Management*, 4th ed. (Englewood, CO: Libraries Unlimited, 1993). See especially the chapter "Principles of Control," which includes budgeting techniques. See also Murray Martin, *Academic Library Budgets* (Greenwich, CT: JAI, 1993). This volume is part of the "Foundations in Library and Information Science" series.

   A continuing source of financial information is a quarterly journal dedicated exclusively to library financial problems and solutions: *The Bottom Line: Managing Library Finances*, at

60/62 Toller Lane, Bradford, West Yorkshire, England BD8 9BY, tel. 44-1274-777700, fax 44-1274-785200. This journal, formerly called *The Bottom Line: A Financial Magazine for Librarians*, was originally published by Neal-Schuman Publishers. *The Bottom Line* continually seeks article contributors; see a recent issue for details.

A book on how a variety of libraries coped with various budget challenges is Linda F. Crismond, ed., *Against All Odds: Case Studies on Library Financial Management* (Fort Atkinson, WI: Highsmith, 1993). Sections include Financial Structure and Funding Sources, Campaigns and Coalitions, Distribution of Resources, Cutback Management, and Borrowing from Business.

A helpful piece on preparing a budget for the first time is Alan Hall, "Budget Preparation," in Bill Katz, ed., *The How-To-Do-It Manual for Small Libraries* (New York: Neal-Schuman, 1988): 84–90.

2. An interesting look at how formula budgeting methods are used for materials at Central Missouri State University is described in: Mollie Niemeyer, et al., "Balancing Act for Library Materials Budgets: Use of a Formula Allocation," *Technical Services Quarterly* 11:1 (1993): 43ff.

3. The small New England town with a program budget lists "performance measures" for each program. For Reference, for instance, two of six performance measures are "to achieve a 95% satisfaction rate for solving patrons' information needs" and "to maintain reference standards by surveying the quality and currency of information sources in all possible formats" (including CD-ROM and Internet service).

4. For an in-depth discussion of program budgets (e.g., direct versus indirect costs, fixed versus variable costs, intermediate costs, depreciation, amortization, the cost of space for each program) see Barbara M. Robinson, "Costing Question Handling and ILL/Photocopying: A Study of Two State Contract Libraries," *The Bottom Line* 4:2 (Summer 1990): 20–25.

5. A straightforward, how-to summary of zero-based budgeting is Carol Hodlofski, "Zero-Based Budgeting: A Tool for Cutting Back," Bottom Line 5:2 (Summer 1991): 13–19. The piece points out its advantages and disadvantages, presents strengths and weaknesses, outlines a history of ZBB, gives sample forms, and provides a bibliography.

A staff member at the Special Libraries Association points out: "We use a zero-based budget in combination with program and line-item budgets. We use zero-based as a *comparison.*"

6. I originally compiled these "decision package statement" queries for the Special Libraries Association.

7. A professor of library/information science recently quipped that her "Collection Development" course was really "teaching another kind of zero-based budgeting. You look at your users," she said, "figure out as best you can what they need, you put some costs on those needs, and then you rank those needs in priority order. That's what collection development is all about."

8. Two helpful books on budgeting are Richard S. Rounds, *Budgeting Practices for Librarians*, 2d ed. (Chicago: American Library Association, 1994); and Ann E. Prentice, *Financial Planning for Libraries*, 2d ed. (Metuchen, NJ: Scarecrow, 1996).

3 MEASURING OURSELVES

This chapter suggests four methods of "measuring" a library and its services. The first is to know your numbers—measure your library against those numbers. The second method addresses formal library standards, since most libraries are measured against at least one set of standards. The third method incorporates informal "rule-of-thumb" standards, few of which can be substantiated but some of which can be extraordinarily helpful. The fourth measurement technique involves keeping and using statistics about the library.

The most effective budget presentations are made by those who have taken their own measure. Measuring one's own library can be tricky and is usually inexact, but those who have done their best to measure themselves speak with authority, with clarity, with assurance.

There are ways, none totally perfect, of measuring a library. Knowing the appropriate numbers contributes a lot. There are formal standards for many—but not all kinds—of libraries. There are increasing numbers of informal, "rule-of-thumb" standards. Statistics help. If we look hard enough, we can usually find some way to measure ourselves.

KNOW YOUR NUMBERS

In evaluating one's library, it is necessary to determine the numbers—the numbers of one's own library, the numbers of the community the library serves, as well as the numbers of libraries similar to your library. (Note that questions about numbers that are asked in the following paragraphs are listed individually in the Questions to Help You Focus section at the end of this chapter.)

If your library is a public library, what is the population of the community served? What are the demographics, how many people are in each age group, how wealthy (or poor) are community members? How many square feet are in the library? What is the collection size? Annual circulation? Branches? Budget? Endowments? What is the total budget of the community served—the village, town, city, county? What percent of this budget goes to support your library? What is the fiscal year of your community, and therefore of your library?[1] In what year was your library's building built, remodeled, added on to? What are characteristics of similar libraries? The list can go on seemingly endlessly.

If your library is an academic library, what is the population being served—students, faculty, staff, alumni, community? Is your library part of a consortium? How many academic departments are at your institution? To what level are degrees awarded, and in which departments? Are there departmental libraries? How many square feet does the library encumber? How large is the collection? What are circulation statistics? What is the all-over budget for the academic institution? What is the budget for the library? Are there library endowments? When does the academic fiscal year begin, when does it end? What is the building's age and condition? How do you compare to libraries in similar academic settings? And so forth.

If you manage a school library, how big is the school, how many grades, how many students in each grade? How many faculty are there? Are there classroom collections? What is the square footage? What is being taught at your school? What are the library's budget, school's budget, per-pupil budget, community budget? What is the fiscal year? What are the libraries like in similar schools? And others.

If you work in a special library, what is the structure of your company—nonprofit (also known as not-for-profit), corporation, partnership, proprietorship?[2] If your company is publicly held, on which stock exchange is stock traded? What is the share price? What are the numbers in the annual report? What is the gross income of your firm, what is the operating profit? What is the fiscal year? What is your library's budget? Is there charging out, charging back? How many employees, how many departments? How many square feet in the library? What about branches, overseas offices? You'll come up with your own questions, too.

What accounting method does your library use—cash or accrual? If a library orders a $50 book in April, the book arrives in May, and is paid for in June, libraries using cash accounting consider the $50 as a June expense—that is, when the $50 was actually spent. Libraries using accrual accounting consider the $50 an April expense: once an order is placed, the money is "spent." Most libraries use the accrual method. However, more libraries are using credit cards and payment by check with the order; paying by invoice after the book has been received is extremely expensive, both for the vendor and for the library. These days, often there are two prices—the lower for "payment with order" (credit card or check), the higher for "payment upon invoice."

There are, of course, advantages and disadvantages to both the cash system and the accrual system. Prudent financial managers keep track of finances using both methods.

FORMAL STANDARDS

Most libraries are covered by at least one set of standards, with those used depending on the kind of library and on geographical location. Whether you agree with them,[3] you should be familiar with whatever standards are appropriate for your library.

For instance, *Standards for Public Library Services to Children in Massachusetts* (1995) was approved by the Massachusetts Library Association in 1987 and has been continuously revised for currency. Libraries in Massachusetts have used these standards to help justify children's librarian positions, to guide construction of children's facilities, and to document eligibility for children's services grant projects. Like most standards, these are qualitative, not quantitative. They address philosophy of service, the services themselves, staff, collections, programs and facilities. And yet with many standards, the only reference made to money, to budgets, uses the deliberately vague phrase of "sufficient funds."[4]

There are standards in some states, for instance, which require that a certain percentage (often 30 percent) of a public library's materials budget be for children's materials. However, a student doing research on one state's services to young people in public libraries found variations between 10 percent and 40 percent in actual expenditures; she could find no state standard at all. Some states have standards about percentages of library budgets that must be spent on materials in order to qualify for state aid.

The current national standards for school library media centers feature an appendix, "Budget Formulas for Materials and Equipment." In planning the budget for next year, one suggested formula includes what was spent on media this year, variation in student population, library materials attrition (weeding, out-of-dateness, loss), and inflation rate. Another formula more nearly approaches a line-item budget, with lines developed depending on size of school, condition of current collection, replacement of lost items, and similar aspects.[5]

Most states also have school library budgeting guidelines within which each community sets its own guidelines. Massachusetts, for instance, suggests that minimal library materials involve spending for each pupil at one-third of 1 percent of the average per-pupil expenditure, average spending amounts to two-thirds of 1 percent, and that "exemplary" expenditures total the full 1 percent.[6]

Most academic libraries have quite specific standards. In some academic libraries, the number of serials subscribed to or the ratio of serials subscription dollars to the materials budget are dictated by accreditation standards. "Standards for Community, Junior, and Technical College Learning Resources Programs" say: "An ample and stable budget should be based either on a percentage of educational and general budget totals for the institution . . . or based on a dollar amount per full-time student equivalent." Also: "All directly related revenues such as fines, payments for lost and damaged materials, sale of unneeded items, and student use fees, should be used solely for the support of collection, services, and activities of learning resources programs."[7]

Using available standards,[8] an academic institution can also estimate optimum library square footage. Standards call for a basic collection of 85,000 volumes (whatever a "volume" is), plus 100 per full-time equivalent (FTE) faculty member, plus 15 more per FTE student, plus other allowances based on numbers of fields and at what level (350 for undergraduate majors or minors, 25,000 for each doctoral field). Optimum square feet are based on optimum volume counts.

The first standards for special libraries were published in 1964 and addressed objectives, staff, collection, services, physical facilities and budget. These standards pointed out that staff salaries should account for 60 to 79 percent of the special library's budget; however, "some variation in ratios must be expected for those special libraries that may receive a large percentage of their materials without cost." Also: "The final budget is the joint responsibility of the library administrator and the administrator's immediate superior. . . . The administrator maintains close liaison with the accounting department or business office of the parent organization."[9]

The American Association of Law Libraries (AALL) issues standards for Appellate Court and for County Law Libraries; the library budget should be "separate and distinct" from the rest of the budget, the budget should contain "adequate funds" for staff and materials, and the librarian is reponsible for preparing, presenting and managing the budget.[10]

The Medical Library Association Inc. has minimum standards for health science libraries in hospitals: appropriate services, collection, and staffing are described for each hospital size, and presumably budgets can be derived from these descriptions.[11]

Standards of any sort are exceedingly difficult to prepare and even harder to write for any kind of library or library activity. Tempers tend to be short, feelings run high, everyone has an opinion. No matter how well standards are prepared and written they will, to some, be "wrong." This author is currently trying to work with COSAC (Committee on Standards and Credentials) for AIIP (Association of Independent Information Professionals). As of this writing, AIIP members are performing at least thirty-three different services for clients. Given this breadth, how can AIIP set standards? Should standards be set at all? How can any member be "credentialed"? How can COSAC move forward? Or should COSAC simply disband? At the moment, there are no clear answers. Grappling with any sort of standards is not easy.

RULE-OF-THUMB STANDARDS

Rule-of-thumb standards are based upon experience. The longer one works in the library world, therefore, the more "rule-of-thumb" standards one seems to accumulate.[12] They are informal, practically impossible to document, and occasionally inaccurate, yet surprisingly most cut close to truth. Rule-of-thumb standards usually are shared orally, sometimes furtively, occasionally jubilantly; rarely are they written down. Eagerly sought by newcomers and old hands alike, rule-of-thumb standards are benchmarks that no one can prove, yet almost everyone uses.

For instance, there is wide variation of perceptions regarding how many original cataloging decisions can be or should be made by an individual cataloger in an hour. Rumors in academia range between four an hour to four a day.[13]

Other rule-of-thumb standards apply to prices and price increases. In general, serial prices rise exponentially faster than do book prices. Prices fluctuate constantly, and must continually be monitored. Rules of thumb for price increases: 15–16.5 percent per year for serials (more for foreign titles), 7 percent per year for books. This rule of thumb has real implications for research and development libraries, which have heavy serials holdings.[14]

It is important to remember that all standards—formal and informal—must be taken with a grain of salt, and yet these standards cannot be ignored. With that in mind, here *caveat emptor*, and use these as you can.

Many library managers accept that:

- The cost of purchasing equals the cost of processing, i.e., the technical services budget equals the book budget.
- Twenty percent of library materials account for 80 percent of usage. (This is known as "the Pareto principle," named after the nineteenth century Italian economist, Vilfredo Pareto, who pointed out that 20 percent of facts are critical to 80 percent of outcome.)
- Library budgets often have cost break-downs of about 60 percent for personnel, 20 percent materials, 10 percent supplies, and 10 percent all else.

Some academic librarians note that:

- If at least 4 percent of the college's budget goes to the libraries, you would probably want your child to go to that college.

- Academic departmental library budgets can vary widely. A guest lecturer at my Simmons budget class was director of a departmental library at a local university. He had kept track of what percentage each academic department with its own library devoted to that library. The variance was great: 1.97%, 2.61%, 5.76%, 5.82%, 10.86%, 11.66% and 14.0%.
- Gifts should be accepted cautiously: adding gift books to college library collections is absurdly expensive. (A recent student team used classic cost-finding techniques to discover that it cost $17.78 to add a gift book to a student's own college library. At the time, many librarians found this figure low.)

Quite a few school library consultants say:

- All school libraries lose at least 1 percent of their materials each year; many school libraries lose much, much more.
- According to one library consultant (who requests anonymity) in 1995, school library materials budgets were about $10 per pupil per year.
- Another consultant (who also asks to remain anonymous) says that, in 1995, school library materials budgets equalled about 6/10th of 1 percent of the per-pupil cost.

Some public librarians have said:

- A public library's budget generally runs between 1 percent and 2 percent of the municipality's budget.
- In these days of networking and resource sharing, the term "population served" can be highly misleading for public libraries: increasingly, people cross borders to get to a good library.
- "Common knowledge" in precomputer work-station days was that there "should be" between 0.7 and 1.0 square feet per person allowed for the public library population served (however this is computed). However, a Lexington, Massachusetts, 1995 study of 17 nearby public libraries showed a range of between 0.53 square feet and 2.91 square feet. The average square footage was 1.2 square feet.

In the case of special libraries:

- Expenditures are rumored to be between 0.5 and 5 percent of the employer's after-cost-of-sales revenues. Consultants to special libraries consider this percentage in formulating advice for their client, especially if special library expenditures are below 1 percent.

- In 1993, special libraries cost $640 per year per "professional" at the company served, according to Jose-Marie Griffiths and Donald King.[15] Mr. King later said in a private telephone interview, that "this figure varies a *lot* with economies of scale."
- In September 1994, the average special library materials budget was $283,400 per year. Of these, 95 percent used CD-ROMs, 83 percent used online services, 72 percent used the Internet. [16]

As for law libraries:

- A rule of thumb is that between $2,000 and $2,500 per year per attorney in private law firms is spent for law library materials. It doesn't seem to matter whether those dollars are Canadian or U.S.
- In private law firms, the library's materials budget (i.e., without salaries) is said to be approximately 1 percent of the firm's total revenues. Total revenue figures in private law firms are usually securely held proprietary information: this rule-of-thumb standard is at best a guess.
- In public law libraries (such as county law libraries), approximately 30 percent of users are representing themselves in upcoming court cases, and they generate 75 percent of reference questions.

STATISTICS

Virtually all librarians collect statistics about their libraries.[17] Many relate these statistics to their budgets.

Many statistics are now kept automatically. An "invisible eye" counts bodies coming into and going out of the library. Electronic systems count how many of what kinds of materials go out and come back. Patrons who keep materials longer than they should are identified by computer (although in most cases a human being still must track them down).

When tracking statistics by hand, be very clear how your statistics are to be kept and make it very easy for library staff to collect statistics. Use whatever tools seem easiest—pencils, forms, check marks, spreadsheets. Bring statistics up-to-date frequently; do not wait until the end of the month, the end of the quarter, the end of the year—catching up at the end of the week is hard enough. Consistency and continuity are paramount: statistics kept for at least three years are most useful.

Collect whatever statistics seem appropriate to your library and its budget. Some investigations to consider might include:

- number of telephone inquiries
- average response time and cost of this time
- average time a telephone patron is kept "on hold"
- number of online searches, average cost of search, and cost of time to do the search
- number of online searches compared to last year's number, and how the cost compares
- how many requests come in per hour
- how many requests come in per year
- how many requests come in per staffer per year
- how many questions could *not* be answered
- how much users really use the library, per type of request, per department, and so on
- new technologies—how much time do reference staff spend teaching patrons, and what is the cost of this time

Keeping statistics is important, even if they are collected on a sampling basis rather than day in and day out (some libraries declare the first day of the month to be "statistics day"). But even more important is how statistics are used. We may be tempted to use our statistics to prove to management how good we are, or busy we are, or overworked or understaffed we are. But, the statistics we provide to management—the school principal, the town manager, the financial vice-president—must be significant to management. Remember that most managers to whom we report are not librarians, and use management language, not library language. If there is a cataloging backlog, for instance, use "inventory control" (i.e., letting material out without being cataloged), or "costly duplication" (i.e., we won't know what we have unless it is cataloged). Other library jargon to avoid includes terms such as "vertical file," "technical services," "ILL," and "OCLC."

A recent example of using statistics to make managerial decisions has been documented by a company that makes and sells cookies through franchised dealers.[18] Extensive statistics are constantly kept, and are entered into a database. Franchisees come to work in the morning, turn on their computers, and are given realistic sales goals based on location, day of week, weather, whether school is on vacation, and the like. All this translates into how much cookie dough to mix up, how many new bakers to interview, and even how to know when sales are lagging—and when they do lag, free broken cookie bits are passed around outside on the sidewalk to lure customers.

Statistics, like standards, must be used with care. Remember that every library is different. There are no one-size-fits-all standards or statistics.[19]

QUESTIONS TO HELP YOU FOCUS

KNOW YOUR NUMBERS

   A. Review chapter 1, "Numbers, Your Library, and You," and review the questions in that chapter.

   B. For any library:

      What is the fiscal year of your organization?
      When was your library built, remodeled, added on to? How many square feet does your library encumber?
      Collection(s)? Circulation?
      Current budget?
      Method of accounting (cash or accrual)?
      What are the numbers of libraries similar to yours?

   C. If your library is a public library:

      What is the population of the community served?
      What are the demographics of this public?
      How many branches are there?
      Do you have any endowments?
      What is the budget of the community served?
      What percent of this budget goes to the library?
      Are there similar libraries nearby?
      Are there other numbers you should know?

   D. If your library is an academic library:

      Describe the population served—students, faculty, staff, alumni, community.
      Is your library part of a consortium?
      How many academic departments are at your institution?
      To what level are degrees awarded? In what departments?
      Are there departmental libraries?
      What is the budget of your college/university?

What percent of this budget goes to the library?
Are there other numbers you should know?

E. If you manage a school library:

How big is the school?
How many grades, how many students in each grade?
How many faculty?
Are there classroom collections?
What are your school's budget, per-pupil budget, community budget?
Are there other numbers you should know?

F. If you are in a special library:

What is the structure of your organization?
If stock is traded, on which stock exchange?
What is the share price?
What are numbers in the most recent annual report?
What percent of the operating budget is your library?
Do you charge out, charge back, charge fees?
Are there branches, overseas offices?
Are there other numbers you should know?

FORMAL STANDARDS

A. What formal standards apply to your library? If needed, procure a copy of those standards.
B. How does your library measure up to those standards?

RULE-OF-THUMB STANDARDS

A. Reread the rule-of-thumb standards presented in chapter 3.
B. Do any apply to your library?
C. With which do you agree, with which do you not agree?
D. Are there rule-of-thumb standards you could share/contribute?

STATISTICS

A. What statistics does your library keep?
B. How are these statistics used?

USING STANDARDS AND STATISTICS

A. What changes will you make or action will you take regarding standards or statistics?
B. Do you have unanswered questions about standards and/or statistics? What are these questions? To whom can you go for answers?

NOTES

1. As individuals, we use the "calendar year" as our fiscal year—our accounting year ends officially on December 31 and starts again on January 1. Other entities may use other fiscal years. The U.S. government, for instance, ends its year on September 30 and starts the next year on October 1. FY stands for Fiscal Year. For the U.S. government, FY1998 (or FY98) begins on 1 October 1997 and ends on 30 September 1998.

2. This discussion about for-profit and nonprofit, about corporations and partnerships and proprietorships, uses U.S. terminology. Other English-speaking countries' terminologies are slightly different. Briefly, a nonprofit special library might be located in a hospital, at a museum, or at an association. In the for-profit sector, a corporate special library might be in a consulting firm, manufacturing plant, or insurance company. Libraries in partnerships might be in law firms or advertising agencies. There are, however, few formal special libraries in proprietorships which are owned by one person and are often called "dba"s ("doing business as . . . "—as in "Alice Sizer Warner dba The Information Guild.")

3. At least one educator has grave concerns about standards as applied to schools, saying "Are 'standards' to apply to the school or to the students or both? . . . If the 'end' is reached, the means don't make any difference." Theodore R. Sizer, "Rethinking 'Standards'" (a monograph), available for $1.00 from Coalition of Essential Schools, Box 1969, Brown University, Providence RI 02903.

4. As of this writing, *Standards for Public Library Services to Children in Massachusetts* is available for $10 from The Massachusetts Library Association, 707 Turnpike Street, North Andover, MA 01845, tel. 508-686-8543, fax 508-685-4422. In general, information about public library standards is available from the various state library agencies (see note 5 in chapter 4).

5. American Association of School Librarians and Association for Educational Communications and Technology, *Information Power: Guidelines for School Library Media Programs* (Chicago: American Library Association, 1988). A revision is due in 1998.

    Since 1983, studies of school library media centers' (LMCs) expenditures have been published approximately every two years in *School Library Journal*. See, for example, Marilyn L. Miller and Marilyn L. Shontz, "The Search for the School

Library Dollar," *School Library Journal* 41:10 (1 October 1995): 22–23. Authors report: "Book spending stagnant, nonprint resources catching up. . . . Because each level [of school] discarded at least as many books as they bought, little progress is being made in even maintaining, much less expanding collection size. . . . Median expenditures for schools enrolling more than 2,000 students total $8,500. Of that $8,500, or $11.44 TME per pupil, $3.43 is spent for books . . . 60% of respondents use [cable television]. . . . Teachers and students in 25% of the LMCs have Internet access and e-mail."

For those readers specifically interested in school LMCs, check Betty Morris, John T. Gillespie and Diana L. Spirt, *Administering the School Library Media Center*, 3d ed. (New York: Bowker, 1992), especially the chapter called "Budget," pp. 132–78.

6. To get a copy of school library standards in the Commonwealth of Massachusetts, contact the Massachusetts School Library Media Association for *Standards for School Library Media Centers in the Commonwealth of Massachusetts*, 1988. Copies are available for $5 from Margaret A. Drew, 60 Myopia Road, Hyde Park, MA 02136. In preparation for a November 1995 MSLMA conference program on standards, attendees were to indicate level of agreement/disagreement with the statement: "The library media program's budget will be 5% of the per pupil expenditure for the school system exclusive of salaries and special education expenses."

7. Association for Educational Communications and Technology (AECT), "ACRL Standards: Standards for Community, Junior, and Technical College Learning Resources Programs," *College and Research Libraries* 55:9 (October 1994): 572–85.

8. *Standards for College Libraries* (Chicago: American Library Association). Make inquiry also from ALA's Headquarters Library and Information Center for additional standards and budget information as well as for a listing of standards and guidelines on deposit at the Library and Information Center.

9. "Objectives and Standards for Special Libraries" is available from SLA, 1700 18th St. NW, Washington, DC 20009, tel. 202-234-4700, fax 202-265-9317.

10. Details are available from the American Association of Law Libraries, 53 West Jackson Boulevard, Suite 940, Chicago, IL 60604, tel. 312-939-4764, fax 312-431-1097.

11. Information is available from Medical Library Association, Inc., Suite 300, Six North Michigan Avenue, Chicago, IL, 60602, tel. 312-419-9094, fax 312-419-8950.

12. I collect rule-of-thumb standards and would welcome reactions to, refutation of, or expansion of those expressed here, as well as comments and contributions. Alice Sizer Warner, Information Guild, Box 254, Lexington, MA 02173, tel. 617-862-9278, fax 617-863-8678, e-mail 75450.250@ compuserve.com.

13. An article that gives a formula to use when figuring costs of cataloging is ALCTS Technical Services Cost Committee, Association for Library Collections & Technical Service, American Library Association, "Guide to Cost Analysis of Acquisitions and Cataloging in Libraries," *ALCTS Newsletter* 1:5 (1991): 49–52.

14. A number of organizations monitor and publish price trends. *Library Journal* publishes annual articles about prices. Several of the larger library subscription agencies publish annual price predictions and reports. The American Association of Law Libraries (AALL) and *The Bowker Annual* are sources for legal publications costs.

15. *Special Libraries: Increasing the Information Edge* (Washington, DC: Special Libraries Association, 1993).

16. These special library figures are based on a survey of readers of *Corporate Library Update* 3:17 (15 November 1994): 2.

17. See: Mark Smith, *Collecting and Using Public Library Statistics: A How-To-Do-It Manual for Librarians* (New York: Neal-Schuman, 1996). See also the following article: Allan D. Pratt and Ellen Altman, "Live by the Numbers, Die by the Numbers," *Library Journal* 122:7 (15 April 1997): 48–49. The article is subtitled "Attributing too much importance to [public] library statistics can be hazardous to your job."

18. Statistics are used managerially by Mrs. Field's Inc., 333 Main Street, Park City, UT 84060, tel. 801-649-1304, fax 801-645-2223.

19. At least one library scholar decries our libraries' reliance on statistical measures: see Jerry D. Campbell, "Getting Comfortable with Change: A New Budget Model for Libraries in Transition," *Library Trends* 42:3 (Winter 1994): 448–59. Abstract: "The existing library budget model is not adequately assisting libraries in coping with the changes of the electronic information revolution. A more flexible transitional model that focuses on effective systems to manage change is presented." Specifically, the author feels it "would be helpful if libraries would discontinue comparing budgetary ratios and statistics for awhile. . . . [C]omparative statistics help hold our budgets in an unfortunate stasis. . . . In practice, statistical standings are far more important in our current bud-

geting practices than is user satisfaction. . . . [The] transitional library budget should have as few standard ratios as possible . . . [to] encourage libraries to make whatever creative changes are necessary to serve their users with the best services, resources, and technologies possible."

4 ALTERNATE RESOURCES: GRANTS AND ENDOWMENTS

This chapter is about two kinds of monetary gifts libraries receive: grants and endowments. Money in the form of a grant is usually for a specific library-related purpose and is spent soon after its receipt. Endowment money, however, is invested so it can provide a regular income to the library. Investment income, either all or part of it, is spent each year, year after year, for the benefit of the library. Sometimes income from endowment money is spent as specified by those who established the endowment; other endowment income is spent as seems most appropriate.

GRANTS

Most grants come from one of three sources: corporations, foundations, or "the government" (however it is defined).

In general, corporate donations support/enrich the mutual local community. Examples include uniforms for the local softball league, sponsorship of the home-town parade, tree planting in the parks. Usually the purpose of a corporate donation is to create and to conserve a stable, good community.

Foundations are set up under Internal Revenue Service (IRS) laws, which allow foundations to distribute money so as to further the foundation's stated mission. Many foundation donations (as opposed to corporate) aid and encourage agents and agencies of change and put the foundation "on the cutting edge" of social issues. Some foundations support social or community services, others simply underwrite specific interests of the donors. All foundation funds must be "in the public interest." Examples include recognizing exceptional merit in specific arts; sending students, doctors, "ambassadors" to specific geographic areas; building museums and memorials.

In general, government money (federal, state, or local) is given to support governmental initiatives and legislation. For example, Fulbright scholars, Small Business Administration loan programs, tax waivers in metropolitan "business initiative" zones, are all governmentally funded.

When applying for a grant of any sort, it is crucial first to know your own organization—its history, its accomplishments, its problems, and its goals. Be able to define your project. Know what you are now looking for: isolate a doable, possible project—a project your organization could accomplish if/when money becomes available. Be able to talk about this project easily, simply, and convincingly—use laymen's language, not library jargon.

Determine the amount of money you seek. Be able to explain exactly what the money will be used for. Define all the benefits of your project. Be able to explain how doing this project furthers the organization's goals. If possible, be able to explain how doing this project might benefit others (such as your community, other communities, individuals such as youth or immigrants or elders, other organizations).[1]

The next step is to identify potential sources of funding. First, check grants-applied-for and grants-received records within your own organization. What worked? What didn't? What can be learned from the organization's history? (This seemingly obvious recommendation is made here due to the fact that it is often a newly hired individual who is given the task of seeking fresh money for a library. This individual may not know a library's background and track record.)

Check sources of corporate donations, local as well as national and international. Information might come from state or local business associations, local/state utilities companies, banks, Rotary Club, and other business clubs.[2] Also check information (publications, databases, and the like) available from The Foundation Center, 79 5th Ave., New York NY 10003, tel. 212-620-4230. Ask them for referrals to information sources in your state and in your particular area.

Check the office of your state's attorney general (AG) for data on IRS Form 990, which is filed with the IRS each year. A copy is filed at the AG's office in the state in which the grant recipient is located and can be viewed by the public. From this file can be determined who, in a particular state, received grants and from which grantors. When? How much? Looking at Form 990 can be a good source of information about smaller grants and grants from smaller foundations.

When actually ready to apply for a grant, make a careful inquiry of the potential grantor, explaining briefly what you seek and why. Does your project seem to match the grantor's guidelines? If so, ask for: (a) the grantor's most recent annual report, (b) guidelines for grant applications (known as "grant guidelines"), and (c) a list of projects recently funded by the grantor. Some grantors will also send copies of successful grant proposals.

When materials are received from the granting agency, check the dollar range: are you in the grantor's ball park? Check the grantor's recently funded projects: is yours similar and appropriate? Cull the grantor's annual report to determine exactly what language, what words and phrases (often called "operative phrasing") are appropriate. Write down the list of the grantor's operative phrasing terms.

The next step is to write the application for the grant. It is crucial to use the operative phrasing list as the skeleton for the proposal. Check grant guidelines for such aspects as length, format, and forms. How many copies must be submitted? Do you need to provide supporting documents? Do *exactly* as the grant guidelines say; present your project in the grantor's terms.[3]

Unless specifically indicated to the contrary, mention the level of funding sought at the beginning of the application (usually the first paragraph of an application is called an "executive summary"). Budget breakdowns, details, and schedules usually belong on the last pages.

Make sure that, while describing your project, you also tell the grantors exactly what they want to know, preferably using their words (i.e., operative phrasing). Make it *easy* for them to read your application, to fit your ideas into their framework—to match your project with their goals.[4]

Assuming the grant application is successful and the library receives the requested grant money, thank the donor—in writing. (Our mothers knew what they were talking about when they told us always to write thank-you notes!) Be scrupulous about meeting all the grantor's timelines (for grant activity, schedules, reports, budget, and so forth). Drop them a note once in a while telling them how things are going.

Write articles for your organization's newsletter and for your local newspaper, mention the grantor prominently, send copies of these articles to your grantor (unless the grantor requests that there be no publicity). Be ready and willing to write articles for the grantor's own newsletter or other publication: be a visibly grateful recipient of the money. Be meticulous about project-end reporting requirements. File tax documents (see earlier discussion of Form 990). Keep in touch, keep the door open between your organization and the grantor. Keep building the library's reputation and setting the scene for future grants.

When seeking government money, check first with the state library office (the exact name varies from state to state).[5] Many state library offices have information about funding sources beyond/outside those funding sources that they themselves administer. In general, federal funds for libraries (primarily public libraries) are distributed via each state's library agency. Be sure to ask for the "calendar for the promulgation of regulations" for the year in which your library wishes to make application for federal funds. This calendar lists all pertinent dates and activities such as public hearings, comments, letters of intent, filing dates, application writing workshops, review panels meetings, and deadlines. Pay careful attention to all these details.

When seeking, and hopefully when receiving, grant money, it is crucial to remember that the money-giving world is small. Everyone knows everyone else. Word about who applies for money, who receives money, and how recipients manage money gets around. Never inflate figures, misrepresent your organization or your project, or mislead funders in any way.

Money attracts money. If one grantor backs a project, others may follow. Some small, private family foundations only grant funds to organizations that other, larger, grantors have singled out as appropriate recipients. (As one small donor who followed the lead of a larger donor said, "They're the kind of company we like to keep.")

Competition for money is keen. Be alert.[6]

ENDOWMENTS

Libraries can learn much about raising endowment money from other types of institutions already involved in the process. Let's look at a New England preparatory school, for instance, that is in the process of trying to raise $6.5 million dollars in endowment funds.[7]

The school knows exactly how much money it intends to raise. While of course any institution will be delighted to accept more money than is beyond its goal, no successful capital fund drive can be open-ended: one must have goals.

This particular school knows how it plans to spend its $6.5 million dollars: $2 million to support teachers, $2 million to support students, and $2.5 million to support programs and facilities—and the school admits the definitions of "programs and facilities" constantly do, and indeed should, change. (Who, for instance, even ten years ago, could have predicted the computer-related expenses the school now faces?) The school's campaign materials give details about the school's current endowment fund, about growth of this endowment fund in past years, and about how this fund compares to those of other comparable schools.

"Named gift" opportunities are listed, including "$10,000 to establish a Named Library Fund." (Incidentally, the amount of $10,000 as a minumum for a named fund is not unusual. For instance, most colleges will not name a scholarship fund in honor of an alumna/us for less than $10,000; $100,000 is more usual. A named University Chair starts at $1 million and is usually $5 million, and there is a standard minimum of an $80 million contribution for a named building, as of this writing.)

Gifts to this school can include the following "planned giving vehicles":

- cash
- matching gifts[8]
- securites
- real estate
- other property
- bequest intentions
- income trusts
- annuity trusts
- pooled income funds (you and your spouse, for instance, receive a high current income from a "pooled income fund"; when you both die, the capital reverts to the school)
- life income plans
- term trusts
- life insurance

When we librarians think of raising money, we think primarily in terms of raising cash; we tend to forget that it may be more convenient or more tax-expedient for the donor, especially the well-to-do donor, to donate something other than cash. Donations of "appreciated securities" may work best. One librarian eager to support her library school regularly gives shares of stock that was given to her by her mother in the 1960s, when the stock cost $15 per share. This stock is now worth $100 a share. Let's assume our librarian wants to give $500 to her school. If our librarian sells five shares of stock to liberate $500 to give her school, the school gets the $500 all right, and the librarian gets to deduct the donation of $500 at income-tax time. Yet the librarian must also, at income-tax time, pay a capital gains tax on the difference between $15 per share and $100 per share—i.e., the amount she "gained" when she sold the stock. The librarian would pay taxes on $85 per donated stock share, or $425. But if the librarian gives the stock directly to the school, the librarian gets to deduct the donation of $500 at income-tax time and without paying a capital gains tax. The school gets the $500 by selling the stock but doesn't have to pay any capital gains tax because it is a non-tax-paying entity.

This sort of contribution is entirely legal. Most established money-raising institutions eagerly seek such donations. And yet this sort of contribution is rarely suggested by a library school or by a library. And when libraries or library schools receive such donations, they seem not to know how to acknowledge the gifts or even what to do with them. We librarians have much to learn about encouraging all manner of charitable donations to our libraries.

Other contributions might be land or buildings, art works, or jewelry. Life insurance policies may be made over, in part or in whole. Donations may be in the form of a bequest in a donor's will, which decreases the size of the donor's estate and therefore its tax rate.

The director of a library with an endowment is responsible for investing endowment money so as to create endowment income. Managing a library endowment is a matter of public trust, a serious business. Library directors usually are not sophisticated investors, but having a library endowment means you have to know about how to make the endowment money grow.

Most libraries with endowment funds find advice of financial managers to be extremely useful. Most endowment-rich libraries invite and listen regularly to volunteer boards made up from the local money-wise community. These boards can be of great assistance in advising the library director about investment details.

Most libraries opt to keep endowment investments on deposit with an investment house rather than to retain paper stock shares, bonds, and the like in a bank safety deposit box. Each investment house customer is assigned an account executive, and this account executive can give helpful advice to the library director. Virtually everyone agrees that library endowment monies should generally be prudently placed in stable, established investments.

The library director generally receives a good deal of mail in connection with the library's endowment investments,[9] including a monthly statement from the library's investment house. Such a statement summarizes monthly activity (such as deposits to the endowment fund, interest income to each investment, outgo spent by the library), and lists each investment in detail (current value, current yield in terms of a percentage figure, and so on).

The library director also receives mail from each company or fund in which the library endowment fund has invested. Among inclusions in this mail are financial statements couched in quarterly and annual reports, invitations to annual meetings, and ballots on which shareholders who do not plan to attend annual meetings may express opinions about how things should be managed.

It takes a bit of practice to understand financial statements, and most library directors have not had the opportunity to learn this skill, so it pays to do a bit of homework.[10]

A financial statement comes in four parts: the balance sheet, the income statement, the cash flow statement, and the statement of shareholders' equity. Most financial statements also include an auditor's opinion. The balance sheet is a financial snapshot of the company on the last day of the time period covered by the financial statement (i.e., the last day of the quarter-year for a quarterly report, the last day of the fiscal year for an annual report). The income statement (also called a "profit and loss statement") shows how the business did during the period. The cash flow statement shows where cash came from and what it was used for during the period. The statement of shareholders' equity tells about the book value of the company during the reporting period. The auditor's opinion is just that: what an independent, outside, auditor thinks about the financial statement and the company it represents. Most readers of financial statements say that auditors' opinions and small-print footnotes to the report are the most revealing.[11]

How one spends an endowment's income may depend on the donor's wishes: you may be limited to specific sorts of materials (of interest to women, for instance, or about the environment, or appropriate for handicapped persons). Endowment income "may be designated for the purchase of rare books, science materials, or for the support of a distinguished lecture or author series. Proposing to use the income from an endowment for 'general operating expenses' is unwise."[12] Prudent endowment managers spend only part of the endowment's income (often half), preferring to reinvest unspent income as capital.

Ideally, endowment income funds can be used to meet changing needs, needs that were not necessarily envisioned when the endowment was set up. At least one public library finds itself using endowment income to purchase money-saving multiyear journal subscriptions; the library is located in a town whose annual library allocation is specifically limited to this-year purchases.

VOLUNTEER!

We librarians are taught little about raising money in library school, and we have much to learn.

A valuable way to gain experience is through volunteering. Most schools and churches welcome money-raising volunteers with open arms. Offer to help elderly people with their finances. Teach (the best way to master a subject!) a one-day, or even a half-day, budgeting class at your community college. Become treasurer of whatever organizations you belong to. Join a money-related committee in your local government.

Be honest both about your lack of experience and your willingness to learn. for it is by doing that we learn.

QUESTIONS TO HELP YOU FOCUS

FOR ALL LIBRARIES SEEKING GRANTS:
  A. Why might a corporation give money to a library?
  B. Why might a foundation give money to a library?
  C. Why might government money be given to a library?
  D. What is the history of applications for, and receipt of, grants in your library?

IF YOU SEEK A FUTURE GRANT FOR YOUR LIBRARY:
  A. Explain your project.
  B. What are your project's benefits to your library?
  C. What are benefits to other libraries?
  D. How much money do you seek?
  E. Who are potential donors?
  F. How do you get hold of the chief librarian of your state's library agency? (See note 5.)
  G. What help is available to your library from your state's library agency?

IF YOU ARE READY TO APPLY FOR A GRANT:
  A. What are the grantor's guidelines?
  B. What is the grantor's operative phrasing?

IF YOU RECEIVE A GRANT:
  A. What steps, step by step, do you take next?

FOR ALL LIBRARIES SEEKING ENDOWMENTS:
  A. What is the difference between an endowment and a grant?
  B. What endowments does your library now have?
  C. What kind of donations, other than cash, might your library seek?
  D. What will you do, step by step, with endowment contributions when you get them?
  E. How might your library spend endowment income?

NOTES

1. For example, some years ago the town of Weston, Massachusetts, received a grant to pay an indexer to create a computerized index for a particular number of years of the local weekly newspaper. The grant details, very wisely, required the indexer to write how-to instructions for the benefit of, and availability to, other indexers of small-town papers. These how-to instructions were kept at what in Massachusetts is called the Board of Library Commissioners (see note 5 below) so that other libraries could themselves create an index to a local paper.

2. For a discussion of partnerships with businesses, see John Berry, "A Good Deal for Both," *Library Journal* 120:20 (December 1995): 6. Corporations, obviously, seek value for their money, and the library must "make certain that the corporate giver fully understands the tremendous value to the corporation in being named the library's partner."

3. In a private communication about raising grant money, a colleague sent a warning. "It would perhaps seem dumb to a grantor if an applicant merely parroted back the grantor's phrasing in a mindless manner. The ideas should obviously mesh, and perhaps even some of the grantor's buzzwords appear; but, for example, to write a conclusion that, in effect, says that your project will conform to their phraseology would be a bit obvious and suspect. What you have to do is to make sure that your project is a serious candidate for fulfillment of the grantor's mission statement."

4. It is extremely important, when applying for grant money, not to use library jargon. The reason why can be discerned from something that happened in New England. In many New England towns, large money expenditures are first considered by the town's Appropriations Committee, and many such committees are made up of community volunteers. One such committee was chaired by the president of a machine tool company, who came to me for clarification of a request made by the local library. "I don't get it," said the committee chair. "Why can't our library make do with some lumber, some two-by-fours?" It seems the library's director had asked the Appropriations Committee for somewhere in the neighborhood of $100,000 "to support the circulation desk"—i.e., for a computerized circulation system. The Appropriations Committee's chair, on the other hand, thought that the circulation desk was falling down, and needed to be

propped up—and why should this propping up cost $100,000?! (The end of the story is that the library in question is now fully computerized.)

5. A list of the library offices in each of the U.S. states is available from COSLA (Chief Officers of State Library Agencies), 167 West Main St. #600, Lexington, KY 40507, tel. 606-231-1925, fax 606-231-1928. Internet addresses for most state librarians are also available from COSLA.

6. Sources of information about grants should be carefully screened for how current they are—the grant-giving world changes constantly. As of this writing, useful sources include:

- materials from the American Library Association, 50 E. Huron Avenue, Chicago, IL 60611, tel. 800-545-2433. A current publication is *The Big Book of Library Grant Money 1996–97*.
- materials from the Foundation Center, 79 5th Avenue, New York, NY 10003, tel. 212-620-4230 or 800-424-9836. Current publications include *National Guide to Funding for Libraries and Information Services, The Foundation Directory, The Foundation Center's Guide to Proposal Writing*.
- Pat Molholt, "Grantsmanship," *Information Outlook* 1:5 (May 1997):13–14. The author is assistant vice-president and associate dean for Scholarly Resources, Columbia University Health Sciences.
- Andrea Lapsley, "Writing Winning Grant Proposals," *The Bottom Line* 8:4 (1995): 38–41. Ms. Lapsley is director of marketing and development for the Houston (Texas) Public Library. The article's emphasis: the funding organization has goals of its own; a winning proposal shows how your program will further those goals.
- "Funding Focus," *American Libraries* 26:11 (December 1995): 1101. ALA's Fund for American Libraries lists twelve guidelines on developing and submitting applications to corporate and foundation resources. Among them: learn as much about the potential funder as possible; make your story compelling; think BIG!; establish a realistic evaluation plan; prepare a realistic budget.
- *Annual Register of Grant Support: A Directory of Funding Sources* (New York: R.R. Bowker). An annual publication; the 1995 edition listed 3,155 U.S. and Canadian grant-making agencies.
- Murray S. Martin, "Gifts, Grants, and Libraries," *The Bottom Line* 8:2 (1995): 37–39.

- The Oryx Press publishes materials about getting grants. 1995 titles included: *Funding Sources for Community and Economic Development, Directory of Grants in the Humanities 1995/96* (9th edition), *The "How To" Grants Manual* (3d edition) (by David G. Bauer), and *Directory of Research Grants 1995*.
- Gale Research, "Private Funding—An Alternative," *Library Journal* 120:6 (1 April 1995): 43. Suggests private funding sources such as the DeWitt Wallace-Reader's Digest Fund, the Otto Bremer Foundation, the Harry Clay Trexler Trust. Gale's *Directory of Corporate Foundation Givers 1995* (The Taft Group) includes more than 8,000 U.S. funding sources, including 3,900 corporate givers.
- Gwen Solomon, "Where and How to Get Grants," *Electronic Learning* 10:1 (January 1991): 16–19. "Budget being squeezed? Maybe a grant can help. Here are grant writing tips, funding sources and directories. . . . If you need money for a technology-based project, there's a good chance you can find a grant to fund it." Discusses federal sources, state funds, foundations, local education funds and corporations.
- Ronald R. Heezen, "Take Money for Granted: Grant Proposals That Work," *Library Journal* 116:18 (1 November 1991): 62–63.
- Peggy Barber and Linda Crow, *Getting Your Grant: A How-To-Do-It Manual for Librarians* (New York: Neal-Schuman, 1992). A step-by-step guide, including worksheets and checklists, sample timetable, and information about foundations.

7. The name of the school is deliberately withheld to protect the privacy of individuals involved.
8. A matching gift is a one-to-one (or greater) contribution by one's employer to selected charities to which the employee chooses to donate. Donors must get a matching gift form from the employer's personnel office and follow directions to initiate a match. Information on matching gifts is available from the National Clearinghouse for Corporate Matching Gift Information, Council for Advancement and Support of Education (CASE), Suite 400, 11 duPont Circle, Washington, DC 20036–1261.
9. It is wise to procure (and to keep up to date) a "Records Retention Timetable" indicating legalities of what to keep and for how long. Such timetables are often available free for the asking from certified public accountants.

10. A good first step is *How to Read a Financial Report*, continually revised and updated by Merrill Lynch. In less than thirty pages we are walked through financial statements of "Typical Manufacturing Company, Inc." (whose senior officers are, incidentally, women). A copy of this publication is available through the broker-of-the-day at any office of Merrill Lynch.

11. An excellent discussion of financial statements appears in Madeline J. Daubert, *Money Talk: Accounting Fundamentals for Special Librarians* (Washington, DC: Special Libraries Association, 1995). *Money Talk* was prepared as a self-study program.

12. Quoted from Jeffrey Krull, "Private Dollar$ for Public Libraries," *Library Journal* 116:1 (1 January 1991): 66.

    Other suggested reading includes: James G. Neal and Lynn Smith, "Responsibility Center Management and the University Library," *The Bottom Line* 8:4 (1995): 17–20. Responsibility Center Management (RCM) is a fiscal management system being exercised at several U.S. universities. This article describes RCM at Indiana University.

5 MORE ALTERNATE RESOURCES: VOLUNTEERS, FUND RAISING

In more library situations than most librarians would care to admit, the library and its budget depend heavily upon the assistance of volunteers. This chapter examines how volunteer labor can effectively be managed.

This chapter also outlines how volunteers have raised and will continue to raise money—nongrant, nonendowment money—for their libraries. Volunteers are voters who can be, and often are, very effective and influential library ambassadors.

In the best of worlds, volunteers enhance the library and its budget yet do not in any way attempt to or appear to supplant the library's budget. Volunteers are voters and as such important people, for voters are any community's decision makers. A library that has satisfied volunteers is a library with a powerful public relations tool. And if a library's budget needs a dramatic increase, the volunteers are first among those who can make that increase happen.[1]

I myself started library life as a volunteer. Way back when our eldest child was in first grade, his school was involved in educational experiments—experiments that we parents wanted very much to know more about. The only way actually to get inside that school for any length of time was to join the volunteers who were starting a library, and library volunteers were welcome to sit with teachers at coffee breaks (which were, as I remember, in the vestibule of the men's room). So, once a week, I paid a babysitter to stay home with our younger children so I could become a school spy. From the teachers we learned what really was going on. (Some of those educational experiments must have worked— that son now has a Ph.D.)

Later, after our town had hired professional librarians to run our local school libraries I and many others became volunteer librarians in the city of Boston. There were almost 200 schools without libraries, and we were sorely needed. Some of us ran libraries, usually one day a week, each week at the same school. Others of us accepted different assignments each week. There were two processing teams whose job was to process books and get them on the shelves. We had the Quality Team (for which I was never good enough) and the Quantity Team, of which I was the chair. I would gather as many volunteers as possible (usually somewhere between five and fifteen), go to a different school each week, set up an assembly line, and process books fast. I shudder now to think of the shortcuts we found acceptable. I shudder even more when I remember how I would charge each volunteer twenty-five cents a week for the privilege of being part of our group; I used the money to buy special tape for attaching book jackets. And yet I look back on all of that volunteering as being possibly the best fun I've ever had.

Eventually, when our youngest child went to high school, I took myself to library school so I could become qualified for what I'd been doing all along as a volunteer. Although I have written a few times about volunteering, I have never again worked in children's libraries; professional life, as so often happens, has taken different turns.

THE WHYS AND HOWS OF VOLUNTEER PROGRAMS

Why do libraries have volunteer programs? Some libraries were started by volunteers, some have always had volunteer programs. Friends of the Library groups often start and manage volunteer programs. Some programs begin when money becomes available to pay a volunteer coordinator (such as at the public library in Providence, Rhode Island, which applied for and received a grant to cover the first two years' salary of its volunteer coordinator). Other volunteer programs start because less funding is available, and the library cannot stay open or provide expected services without volunteers. Special projects, such as installing automation systems, moving to a new location, or opening a branch can trigger a volunteer program. So can tragedy, flood, or fire.

Who volunteers, and why? Both sexes, all ages, volunteer, and for a multitude of reasons. Interestingly, a fast-growing volunteer group is made up of men who have retired but whose wives have not. "Re-entry" people—people coming out of divorce or who are returning to the work world after having treatment for substance abuse—volunteer. Sometimes a court will rule that an individual must perform a certain number of hours of community service, and these people choose to work in a library. Some volunteer to get away from children, others volunteer to be with children: take your pick. Many want to be exposed to the world of computers, or may wish to teach what they know about online databases and off-line CD-ROMs to others who want to learn.

Good volunteer programs do not simply happen, they are made to happen. There is a great deal more to a volunteer program than "free labor": the library must plan, set goals, have a volunteer policy. Someone must be in charge of recruitment, job definitions, application procedures, interviewing, scheduling, creating guidelines and directions, teaching, supervising, and—if necessary—reassigning or even firing volunteers.

The volunteer who hesitates to be "hooked for life" might work well for a finite length of time, such as six weeks. The library that sees that a volunteer is not, for some reason, working out can gently let that volunteer drop out at the end of a six-week period—perhaps by redefining jobs that need to be done in such a way that the volunteer's skills become inappropriate. (Many truly believe "It's impossible to fire a volunteer," and they're wrong.) The six-week schedule seems to help avoid burnout, both among volunteers and professional staff.

Training, both of the professional staff and of the volunteers themselves, is crucial. Logs must be kept, schedules worked out. Personnel and statistical records need attention, evaluations and rewards must be planned. I can't overemphasize the importance of thanking volunteers.

WHAT DO VOLUNTEERS DO OR NOT DO?

What do volunteers actually do? The list is endless.[2]

- Volunteers entice people into the library (host open houses, give library tours).
- Volunteers bring the library outside of itself (show films, read aloud at nursing homes).
- Volunteers make the library look better (decorate, paint, arrange flowers).
- Volunteers work with library materials being acquired (sort gifts, check in magazines).
- They help get materials ready to be used (assign accession numbers, stamp magazines).
- Volunteers handle materials going out on loan (solve reserves mysteries, retrieve newspapers).
- They handle materials coming back to the library (clear bookdrop, load carts).
- When materials are withdrawn or discarded, volunteers stamp and pack discards, price for sale.
- Volunteers work with files, lists, indexes (tally surveys, tidy vertical files).

- Special collections thrive with volunteers who sort histori-cal photographs, maintain scrapbooks.
- Volunteers familiar with machines and AV materials repair microfilm reader, dub videotapes.
- Volunteers familiar with computers input, enter, index, pro-gram.
- Volunteers assist patrons by loading paper in copy machine, giving tours.
- Untold volunteers function as teachers (help with home-work, teach literacy).
- Children and young people benefit from volunteers (who run story hours, craft programs).
- Handicapped people have special needs, so volunteers man-age TTY, check Talking Books returns.
- Volunteers respond to specific staff needs (relieve during vacations, strategy planning).
- Clerical talents of volunteers are used to manage mail, an-swer phone, laminate.
- Volunteers bring artistic skills to a library (signs, posters, bulletin board).
- Volunteers contribute muscles, backs, and legs (shift books, raise flag, paint, scrub).
- Librarians report volunteers do most everything (house-cleaning, fund raising, training).

The list of what volunteers do *not* do bears a remarkable simi-larity to the list of what they *do* do: it all depends on the situa-tion. In some places, unions influence what volunteers may or may not do. Plus, insurance regulations must be heeded. Many libraries protect volunteers from confrontations with the public. Bear in mind that staff and patron confidentiality must be hon-ored, and staff feelings respected. Space may limit what a volun-teer may or may not do.

When it comes to volunteers and volunteer programs, each li-brary is unique. What works in one situation, in one library, may not necessarily transfer itself to another. There are infinite vari-ables; there is exquisite variety.

VOLUNTEERS AND FUND RAISING

A well-run library volunteer program can raise substantial funds for a library—funds that can supplement the normal library bud-get, grant funds, and endowment funds.

Both staff and volunteer effort are usually needed to raise extra funds for a library. So before you start, determine exactly which "pot" gets the money if the library does create extra sources of revenue. In some municipalities, this revenue goes into what is called the municipality's "General Fund" and not directly to the library. And we have heard of academic and school libraries whose extra funding did not go directly to the library. Fund raising by volunteers should never be allowed to supplant public funds: check, double check, get advice before seeking private philanthropy.[3] (In our own old New England town, it is only an "accident of history" that allows our public library to keep its overdue fines—most similar libraries must hand those monies over to the municipality's General Fund. In at least one neighboring town, library fines are passed on, literally, to the dogcatcher.)

The variety of methods used by volunteers to raise extra library funds is extraordinary. Consider:

> Antique bazaar
> Auction of donated goods and services
> Bake sales
> Bumper-sticker sales
> Champagne Disco Dance
> Cookbook
> Day at the Races
> Encouraging corporate matching gifts
> Flea markets, goods donated
> Flea markets, sellers paying to take part
> Handicraft sales
> House tours
> Literary Arts Ball
> Night at the Pops
> Paint donations (including painters)
> Strawberry festival
> Tractor pulls
> Treasure trove antique books
> Victorian garden party (costumes encouraged)[4]

In-kind contributions encouraged by volunteers, and contributed by volunteers themselves, might include:

> Art, prints
> Draperies made to order
> Flowers, plants
> Furniture (including sofa for staff room)
> Globes, maps

Large-print books (often donated by Lions Clubs)
Paint donations, including painting services
Playpens, high chairs

I have found at least two examples of money-raising "Murder in the Library" parties.[5] At the Dublin Branch of the Alameda County Library in California, "author" Agatha Mystry (whose latest book was *Deader Than A Doornail*) "hit the carpet like a ton of books" while the audience toasted her with white muscatel wine. Who committed the foul deed? Appetizers were followed by more wine, things were finally unraveled, a good time was had by all, and the library made money for new books. Another party was held at the Main Library Auditorium in Brockton, Massachusetts. "Lotta Books Returns" had a cast that included Brockton's police chief, the city council president, several city councilors, the brother of the mayor, the high school principal, and the county sheriff—who played the part of an attorney from the firm of "Wight, Wight, Wight and Wong, Wong, Wong." Wine and cheese were served during the first intermission, dessert and coffee during the second, tickets cost $20 each, everyone involved had a roaringly good time, and the library raised $6,000.[6]

CAUTIONARY NOTE

Library money raisers share the same problem with yard salers, church fair people and others who take in cash money: what does one do with the money, with the cash, until the bank opens—either the next day or after the weekend? No individual really wants the unpleasant responsibility of keeping hundreds or thousands of dollars at home.

Retailers have solved that problem by having night-deposit banking arrangements—bagged cash is literally dropped into the bank through a hole in the bank's wall, a hole opened with a key issued to the retailer. Library money raisers can either arrange with a local bank for night deposit or (better yet) can manage to have a banker on the library's money-raising committee.

An alternative that we have seen used many times is to use the services of a large supermarket that is open evening and weekend hours. Supermarkets are equipped to take cash, to lock that cash in their safes, and to issue in exchange a money-order check in the appropriate amount. This service generally costs very little: as of this writing, our local supermarket charges $1.00 for their service of taking in cash and issuing a check.

QUESTIONS TO HELP YOU FOCUS

FOR THOSE LIBRARIES NOW USING VOLUNTEERS:

A. Why does your library have a volunteer program?
B. What do these volunteers do?
C. Who administers the volunteer program?
D. What problems does the volunteer program face?
E. What is the history of volunteering in your library?

FOR THOSE LIBRARIES CONSIDERING STARTING A VOLUNTEER PROGRAM:

A. Why would your library want to use volunteers?
B. How does your regular staff feel about having volunteers?
C. What does your staff hope volunteers will do?
D. Who would administer the volunteer program?
E. How would volunteers be sought?
F. What, specifically, would volunteers do? How much would they do?
G. What, specifically, would volunteers not do?
H. How would problems with volunteers be managed?
I. How would volunteers be rewarded?

FOR LIBRARIES CONSIDERING USING VOLUNTEERS TO RAISE FUNDS:

A. Who gets the money if/when any is raised?
B. What is money being raised for?
C. How will fund raising by volunteers affect financial support from the organization that normally supports the library?
D. How much money does the library hope to raise?
E. Who will the volunteers be?
F. Who on the library staff will supervise the volunteers' efforts?
G. What happens to cash money as it is taken in? Who is in charge of it?
H. How will the library spend money raised by volunteers? Who decides how the money will be spent?

NOTES

1. Recent material on library volunteers includes:

   - See *Library Journal* 121:16 (1 October 1996):16 for a photograph captioned "Book Sales Soaring," wherein Lillian Levin (president of the Friends of the Library) is donating $37,000 to the library, representing money earned via sale of her book, *Planning Library Friends' Book Sales*. The book is available for $10 from Middletown Library Service Center, 786 Main St., Middletown, CT 06457. Checks should be payable to Friends of Connecticut Libraries.
   - Bonnie McCune and Charleszine "Terry" Nelson, *Recruiting and Managing Volunteers in Libraries: A How-To-Do-It-Manual* (New York: Neal-Schuman Publishers, 1995).
   - A "Librarian's Library" notice on p.928 of the October 1995 *American Libraries* cites two recent publications: *Generic Volunteer Orientation Manual: Your Guide to Developing an Orientation Manual for Volunteers* (Albany, OR: Volunteer Support Project, 1995); and Katherine Noyes Campbell and Susan J. Ellis, *The (Help) I-Don't-Have-Enough-Time Guide to Volunteer Management* (Philadelphia: Energize, 1995).
   - Sally Gardner Reed, *Library Volunteers—Worth the Effort! A Program Manager's Guide* (Jefferson, NC: McFarland & Co., 1994). The author is now director of the public library in Norfolk, Virginia.
   - Robert Chadbourne, "Volunteers in the Library: Both Sides Must Give in Order to Get," *Wilson Library Bulletin* 67:6 (June 1993):26–27.
   - Bonnie F. McCune, "The New Volunteerism: Making it Pay Off for Your Library," *American Libraries* 24:9 (October 1993):822+. About the Denver (Colorado) Public Library's program to recruit volunteer workers and match them to approriate library tasks. Almost 57,000 volunteer hours were donated in 1991. Recruitment efforts are directed to seniors, local judicial systems, minority groups, individuals with disabilities, employee groups and other business volunteers. Students are provided with "service learning." Camaraderie among volunteers abounds.

2. The list of what volunteers do is adapted from Alice Sizer Warner, *Volunteers in Libraries II* (New York: R.R. Bowker

Company, 1983):51–53. *Volunteers in Libraries II* reports on what over 500 U.S. libraries were doing—or not doing—with and for volunteers. (Note that this book is out of print and is available only on interlibrary loan.) Included with the book are microfiched volunteer-related documents: application forms, schedules, contracts, job descriptions, etc. Originals from which the microfiche were filmed are on deposit at the Graduate School of Library and Information Science Library at Simmons College in Boston, Massachusetts.

3. An excellent discussion about private fund raising is a previously-cited (note #11, "Grants & Endowments") article: Jeffrey R. Krull, "Private Dollar$ for Public Libraries," *Library Journal* 116:1 (1 January 1991):65–68. Nora Rawlinson, *LJ* editor, adds in the same issue, "More parsley on the potatoes; not the potatoes" on p.67, pointing out experiences in Houston, Texas, where fund-raising efforts were called "The *Enhancement* Campaign for the Houston Public Library" and a restricted fund was set up for money that was raised. Krull, in the body of his article, also advises setting up "an entity separate from the library to receive, administer, and invest any private funds that are raised" (possibly a foundation) and points out that each U.S. state has different laws about this.

   Another article on fund raising: Leonard Kniffel, "Corporate Sponsorship: The New Direction in Fundraising," *American Libraries* 26:10 (November 1995):1023–1026. The classic example of corporate sponsorship happened when Andrew Carnegie built 1,679 U.S. public libraries just before and just after the 1900 turn of the century. Of today's corporate sponsorships, we are warned that "Sponsors don't get everything they want, but you have to realize they are trying to market a product and you're not going to get the money if you don't give them some marketing benefit . . . Corporations approach libraries because it's going to be beneficial to them to be associated with a good cause . . . but it's up to the library to make it a good cause."

4. The listing of volunteers' fund-raising efforts is taken in part from pp.28–29 of *Volunteers in Libraries II*, cited above.

5. The murder parties are described in: Penny and Tom Warner, "Whodunit?," *School Library Journal* 37:12 (December 1991):50. We also found an undated report (probably early April 1995) from the Brockton, Massachusetts, *Enterprise* by Amy Blotcher Guerrero: "Brockton murder mystery performance tests wits of audience."

   Where to buy murder-mystery packets for libraries is described in "Criminal Gain," *American Libraries*, 27:8 (September 1996):25.

6. Other sources on fund raising include:

- Materials from the American Library Association's Library Fundraising Resource Center (50 E. Huron St., Chicago, IL 60611, 800-545-2433 x5045). LFRC's 2–year project, funded by the W. K. Kellog and the Carnegie Foundations, helped create a database, a series of training sessions, and a lending library on fundraising and allied management issues. See also ALA's *Library Fundraising: Models for Success* (1995).
- Kathy Miller, "No-Hassle Ways to Make More Money for Your Library," *MLS* 7:5&6 (1994):7–8. Includes discussion of the following thoughts: rent out available meeting rooms; put out a call for volunteers; seek "sponsors" for purchases; sell unwanted books, records, magazines; ensure you're not losing money on services (such as copy machines); cut back on air conditioning; if you have a "Friends of the Library" program, make sure people know about it; give patrons an easy way to donate.
- Kimberly Taylor, "Getting to Yes: A Fundraising Attitude that Works," *The Bottom Line* 5:4 (Winter 1991–1992):32–34 (cited earlier in chapter I, note #9). "Success in fundraising takes chutzpah. You have to be willing to take risks . . . A lot of people would have us believe that to be a fundraiser, you need an MFA (Master of Fundraising). Not only does such a degree not exist, it shouldn't . . . There are no rules."
- Joan Flanagan, *Successful Fundraising: A Complete Handbook for Volunteers and Professionals* (Chicago: Contemporary Books Inc., May 1991).

6 FEES FOR LIBRARY SERVICES

This chapter discusses libraries that supplement their budgets by shifting payment responsibility directly to those who actually use the library's services. Two methods of doing this—charging back and charging out—are detailed. We cover library fees and fee-based services in academic, public, and special libraries. We also address how to determine fee structures as well as how to market and sell fee-based library services.

The chapter closes with a brief summary of techniques and tips libraries can learn from independent information professionals who charge for their services.

Library services, as all librarians well know, are not free. The issue is, quite simply, exactly who pays for them? Every library seems to be living with one or more interpretations of answers to this question.[1]

INTERNAL TRANSACTIONS: CHARGING BACK AND CHARGING OUT

Two variations of determining who pays, and for what, involve charging back and charging out.

CHARGING BACK

In "charge-back" systems—used primarily in special libraries—the cost of what the library does for an individual, for a project, or for a department within the organization is charged back to the appropriate individual or project or departmental budget. Money does not physically change hands; transactions are reported by the library to the accounting department, and the accounting department makes appropriate adjustments to all the budgets concerned.

The phrase "the cost of what the library does" may be interpreted simply to mean out-of-pocket costs, such as interlibrary loan costs or online connection costs, for which the library is merely recovering out-of-pocket expenditures. However, this phrase may also include costs of the time of library staffers who worked on the project, the cost of space the library encumbers, the cost of library support staff, and so forth. In such cases, cost recovery comes closer to the meaning of another phrase, "full-cost recovery," which is itself open to many interpretations. Exactly how time-related costs are calculated also differs vastly from library to library.

Ideally, both librarians and accountants have input into how charge-back rates are set. Variables might include: librarians' salaries, support staff salaries, benefits, out-of-pocket expenditures, cost of space (library square footage, utilities, air conditioning, and snow shoveling—lists of space costs can be endless). Unfortunately, there are few details in library literature on this issue, and much of what is written is out of date by the time it appears in print.

In a few special libraries, charge-back mechanisms and amounts are matters of open record: at one research facility, a brochure is routinely given to all new employees listing exactly what services are available from the library and at what rate each service will be charged back. Included is everything from borrowing a book (a per-book charge) to online research (hourly charge) to translations (charges depend on the languages). At this research facility, 100 percent of the library budget is recovered from other departments within the organization.

I have discovered a handful of charge-back situations in academic libraries. In one rather extreme case, if the engineering department wants the library to purchase an engineering book, the cost of that book is charged back to the engineering department along with a processing fee.

CHARGING OUT

A special library may be said to "charge out" when library charges are add-ons to clients' bills. A client might come to an organization to buy, for instance, legal or accounting or advertising services. In such cases, whatever work company librarians contribute to the job will be billed to the client—whether the client is aware of it or not. Even though the client has not specifically planned to buy library services, the library is said to have been "charged out" to the client.

How library charge outs are actually managed varies mightily. Usually librarians simply keep track of hours and out-of-pocket expenses and hand these records over to the finance office, which takes care of billings. Most special librarians have rule-of-thumb measurements about charging out their time, ranging from "one-third of the time" (i.e., 2–3 hours a day, an increasingly common number) to 1,700 hours a year.[2]

Even though a great deal of charging out is happening in special libraries, very little is in print in special library literature about this phenomenon. A likely reason is that many special libraries are in competitive businesses and therefore are not free to divulge details about their charging out. (There is, however, much bulletin board-type e-mail on the subject ricocheting around the world.)

EXTERNAL TRANSACTIONS: CHARGING FEES

When a library charges fees, the recipient of the library's services directly pays for the services.

There are seemingly infinite variations among library fees. Most often, fees involve either a transaction (a patron wants the library to do something) or a reaction (the patron has somehow sinned, and the library extracts payment). In these cases, those paying the fees are regular patrons of the library. Fees may involve:

- copy machine services (often provided by an outside vendor, which maintains copy machines and splits income with the library—a constant question for the library involves how much loose change the library will provide to patrons with lots of copying to do)
- facilities rental, rental of space (complete with questions about who is allowed to use space and who might get that space at no charge)
- interlibrary loans (charges, if any, rarely cover true costs of ILLs, a fact being rapidly discovered by librarians)
- overdue books (payment may be forgiven, or partially forgiven, for senior citizens or for the military)[3]
- rental books (usually a per-day charge, and some fast-reader patrons rent books rather than reserve them from the regular collection since it is less expensive)
- rental of works of art (drawings, paintings, etc.—often rental fees are shared with the artist)
- replacement of lost or damaged materials (as with overdues, some patrons are forgiven these charges)
- reserve books (patrons increasingly are reserving the books they want to read via home computer access to the library's catalog)
- sale of blank computer disks (for downloading)
- telephone costs (libraries with in-house pay telephones find them being used heavily on rainy days by traveling sales personnel)

Increasingly, and beyond the "transaction and reaction" listings above, public, academic, and special libraries are establishing formal fee structures for the paying public. Patrons now become clients. Clients must be regular library patrons (live in the public library's area, be affiliated with the university or organization, etc.) or they may otherwise not be able to use the library.

Fees are charged for time, for service, for reimbursement of out-of-pocket costs, and sometimes for permission to enter the premises and use the collection. Fees may be charged for:

- answers to complicated questions
- answers to quick questions
- borrowing materials from the library's collection (especially designed for those who are not otherwise allowed to borrow and for those who want the material delivered rather than to fetch the material themselves)
- CD-ROM searching
- copies of articles (some academic fee-based services say that fully three-quarters of their business comes from document-delivery requests)
- copies of chapters of books
- copyright protection (i.e., clients let the fee-based service worry about dealing with copyright charges)
- interlibrary loans
- manual in-library research
- online searching
- permission to browse the collection in person
- searching that is too complicated for the client to perform at home, at the office, or to have done "by my secretary"
- telephone inquiries
- telephone surveys (especially for clients, such as those in advertising agencies, who do not wish those surveyed to know who is doing the survey)

ACADEMIC LIBRARY FEE-BASED SERVICES

One of the earliest fee-charging schemes in an academic library started at the University of Wisconsin in 1964. Apparently, a far-seeing governor felt businesses in his state would benefit and prosper from available, accessible business information. In that year, when computers as research tools barely existed, there were 539 customers for the fee-based service. In 1986 (with computers), there were 20,000. In 1996, that figure had gone up 25%.

The Georgia Institute of Technology (better known as "Georgia Tech") joined the fee-charging ranks early, as did the C. W. Post branch of Long Island University. Exact numbers of fee-charging academic libraries are hard to pin down, but more than 500 in the United States and Canada have chosen to have themselves counted, and there are probably many more.

One academic fee-based service began when a local bank library closed its doors and gave its entire collection—computers and all—to a nearby graduate school of business administration library. The bank took a huge tax deduction for its donation, and the library used the gift to upgrade its collection. Interestingly, the bank became a captive client of the newly created fee-based service. Within a couple of years, another large special library closed its doors and turned its business over to the college's fee-based service. Currently, graduate students and fee-paying clients (whose numbers keep increasing) are busily using the same facilities.[4]

Often the goal of an academic fee-based institution is "total cost recovery" (whatever that is), plus "fostering good town-gown relations and keeping in touch with our alumni." Town-gown people (i.e., an area's residents and that area's university staff, faculty, and students) must get along with each other, must more than simply coexist. A university library's fee-based service allows nonuniversity residents access to library services: such access has improved many a town-gown situation. The other goal for an academic fee-based service, that of "keeping in touch with our alumni," also has positive results: alumni who are allowed to use their university's library (via a fee-based service) are apt to contribute toward university fund drives.[5]

PUBLIC LIBRARY FEE-BASED SERVICES

Public library fee-based services are hot political topics not only in the United States, but in much of the world. The International Federation of Library Associations (IFLA), as long ago as the mid-1980s, has drawn comparisons between countries with "free" (i.e., tax-supported) public library services and other countries where a charge was made for some services. Conclusions were that any barrier (including fees) would lead to a decline in library use.

Many public libraries, instead of creating fee-based services, have considered the two obvious alternatives: 1) increasing revenues through increased taxes and more gifts and 2) becoming more efficient, especially with the assistance of various computerized services.

The public libraries which do have fee-based services face emotional reactions and criticisms, as well as handling the practicalities involved in managing a fee-based service. Hourly charges vary hugely. Goals are often ill defined. Many public libraries are members of networks, or consortia, and this spirit of so-called cooperation can lead to friction when fee-based services are considered—as well as to "we charge the same as everyone in the consortium does" mindsets.

There are, of course, libraries which seem to have avoided potential problems. I personally visited a public library fee-based service which is located in a large city in the Midwest. At the time of my visit there, the staff knew exactly what the goals of their fee-based service were: to recover (after being reimbursed by clients for out-of-pocket expenses) the salaries (whatever they were) of the three people on the fee-based staff, plus 35 percent of those salaries. The fee-based service was not, at the time, required to recover cost of the space encumbered.

Fees charged by this fee-based service were set with the above goals in mind. Most public libraries are not as clear as to their goals, and as to the relationship between their fees and their goals.

The public library fee-based services that seem to work the best are those which have separate space and staff, as does the midwestern fee-based service that I visited.[6]

FEE-BASED SERVICES IN SPECIAL LIBRARIES

Special libraries may sell a variety of services and products directly to customers and clients. For example, law and accounting firms sell library-access privileges to young company graduates who are starting their own firms, and to recently retired company people who are now independent consultants. One hospital library sold librarian-developed software that was designed to make interlibrary loans easier. More than one association sells access to databases developed from its vertical files and journals.

Fee-charging association libraries tend to have double-tiered fee scales: one fee scale for association members, and another (usually at least double) for nonmembers. Obviously, the goals of charging fees varies from association to association.

Medical libraries have been charging fees for years. Again, goals vary. At least one medical college levies triple-tiered "institutional subscriptions": the highest annual subscription fee is for profit-making institutions, the next level for not-for-profits, and a much lower fee for "individual health professionals." The goal in that case is to provide for nonaffiliated persons with genuine need. Another medical library charges highest fees to "for-profit institutions and information brokers." This medical library's goal (among others) is "to keep other people from making money off us." The library in one of the most prestigious medical clinics charges a very modest flat rate for a medical database search; there is no advertising, searches are carried out only when specifically asked for. Here the goal is to keep good relations with neighboring communities yet not to get sidetracked into full-blown fee-based services.[7]

OUTSOURCING

It is hard to discuss—or even to think of—fees and charges without alluding to outsourcing. Why would a library want to outsource, or contract out, a part or parts of what that library is doing now? Well, for one thing, librarians find there are dramatic increases in what they need to do, primarily in the field of training patrons in the use of the Internet and CD-ROMs. Since these fields are in states of constant flux and have as yet no cohesive standards or searching methodology, library staffers need to make time to teach themselves these changes, to keep up with the changes, to learn how best to teach what they themselves have learned, and to keep learning and keep teaching.

An answer to this dilemma can be to outsource some elements of what used to be the librarians' tasks.

There are at least three varieties of outsourcing. The first variety involves a library outsourcing some part or parts of its activities, such as in the scenario above. Many copy machine services, for instance, are delegated to copy machine providers who may be considered outsourcers. Magazine subscriptions and serials management are frequently outsourced. Book processing is, in many areas, routinely outsourced. We are beginning to hear of book selection, or parts thereof (such as rental books), being outsourced to vendors, to outsourcers.

The second variety of outsourcing happens primarily in special libraries. The library stays in place, but the personnel running the library are employees of the outsourcer: the outsourcer is paid to run the library and to provide information services. Many libraries in agencies of the U.S. government have been outsourced in this manner for years.

In the third variety of outsourcing, also prevalent in special libraries, the library that becomes outsourced simply closes its doors and ceases to exist. The contractor performs information services (answering questions, producing documents, and the like) entirely off site—for a fee.[8]

WHAT TO CHARGE?

When a library first decides to charge fees, there is inevitably an obsessive interest in how much other libraries charge. This interest is understandable, and certainly knowledge of how other libraries manage fees is helpful. But what your library charges does not necessarily depend on what other libraries charge but rather on what the goals are for your library and your community. Desperation may be a trigger, but it cannot be the sole motive. And it is impossible to research what other libraries' goals are: there are literally no published records of other libraries' fee-charging goals.[9]

Decisions must be made. Who will do the fee-based work? Where? Is fee-based work an add-on to the librarians' normal salary? How many hours will the librarian be expected to bill? The goal, as at the above-mentioned midwestern public library, may be to recover three salaries plus 35 percent. This annual financial goal can be reduced to a monthly goal, a weekly goal, a daily goal. How many hours a day can the library bill, will the library bill? What must be charged for these hours to meet the goal?

Yet another goal might be just to provide access to fee-based, in-depth service. Perhaps the library might do the selling but subcontract the actual labor involved, pay the subcontractor, and add a mark-up before delivering to the customer. Would this meet the library's goals? The community's goals?

If the goal is to "compete" with other fee-charging libraries, then perhaps your library's fees should be in line with other comparable libraries' fees. In fact, in a competitive situation, it may benefit you to charge more than others: your library may well then appear to offer better (whatever that means) service.

Most librarians feel they must figure out billing rates all by themselves. In fact, virtually no librarians are without professional financial help. There is in every community a treasurer, a controller, a financial department of some sort: ask for advice, ask for guidance. Some librarians recommend finding out the billing rate of the most junior lawyer in town and using that rate for themselves. Others recommend taking the librarian's hourly wage (including benefits), multiplying that wage by three, and using the result as a billing rate.

It is common for initial prices, whatever they are and however they were arrived at, to be too low. For this reason, it is wise to put a short time limit on prices—probably no more than two to three months. It's advisable not to declare "Prices can change without notice"; better to state, in writing, "Prices valid through [date]."

Variations among charges, at this writing, range from $15 to $200+ per hour. At least one hourly rate seems to have been extremely carefully figured out: $65.47.

MARKETING FEE-BASED SERVICES

Marketing fee-based services is exactly like marketing any other service. Unfortunately, most librarians do not know how to market or how to sell, and they are surprisingly reluctant to learn.

There are at least two excellent newsletters, *Marketing Treasures* and *Marketing Library Services* (*MLS*), that deal with advertising and marketing library services (including fee-based services).[10] And I continue to teach about marketing and selling, and have written frequently about concepts and ideas applicable to the library world.[11]

An even dozen marketing and selling suggestions follow:

1. The easiest sales are repeat sales. Try, when selling, to attract the kind of customer who will keep coming back. Try to avoid "one-shot-type" sales.
2. The next-easiest sales are via referral. Learn to ask for referrals, because a good referral source is a satisfied customer. Ask such customers for names of other potential customers.
3. Be clear as to what it is that you are selling. The information world is infinitely complicated; you cannot sell access to it all.
4. What is your target market? Businesses grossing more than $x-million a year? Professors? Nearby clients? Faraway clients? Alumni? Foreigners? Are there clients you will not accept (such as students)? Be clear.
5. Explain what you are selling in words a nine-year-old would understand. Avoid all information jargon; it will only put off your potential client.[12]
6. Go where the money is, and sell only to those who can afford you. Explain when you expect to be paid and how (many services accept credit cards only, for instance).
7. Emphasize the benefits of what you do, not the process of how you do it. Clients want an answer or to know there isn't an answer. They want their book, their article, their printout, their results. They really don't care how you went about it.
8. Be visible. Go where your clients are, go to their meetings, ask questions at their meetings. Be noticed. Get them used to seeing you. (One librarian advised, "Find out where the local pols' waterhole is, and go there yourself every day.")
9. Write. Write letters to editors. Write interesting articles. Write news releases. Write a regular column for a business

publication. Write and send out a regular newsletter. Tell stories, talk about "questions we were asked this month"—these tales can trigger new questions coming your way.

10. Speak. Be available, be ready. Become known as an excellent speaker: speak for less time than you are asked, be clear, informative, funny. Then take questions and sit down.

11. If you have a brochure, be sure it is simple, handsome, jargon-free. List sample questions you have been asked, tasks you have done. Price lists should be on separate inserts to the brochure. As commented earlier, avoid saying "Prices may change without notice," instead say "Prices valid until [date]."[13]

12. If you are going to exhibit at a trade show, do not exhibit at a library meeting: exhibit where your customers are. (One fee-based service regularly exhibits at automobile trade shows, as this is where that fee-based service's customers are.)

THE INDEPENDENT SECTOR

In the library fee-charging world, much can be learned from entrepreneurial librarians who charge clients for information services. The industry has grown massively from the early 1970s, when there were probably only two dozen information-broker-type services in the United States and Canada; there are nearly 2,000 today.[14]

Within the American Library Association, you can find a group of self-employed librarians called ILERT (Independent Librarians Exchange Roundtable); as of this writing, ILERT members numbered 242. Another source is the consultants' section of the Special Libraries Association's management division; as of now, that section boasts over 600 members. AIIP—Association of Independent Information Professionals—has an international group whose membership as of this writing is more than 800.[15] In addition, there are local groups of self-employed information people in many U.S. areas. Get to know these people. Listen to them, learn from them, use them.

Aside from being valuable contacts, these independent librarians have also taken the time to write about the fee-charging world, which can be of great assistance to those in libraries who are exploring the possibility of charging fees.[16]

QUESTIONS TO HELP YOU FOCUS

CHARGING BACK

A. Does your library charge back?
B. For what, to whom?
C. How are charges computed? What do you feel about how the charges are computed?
D. If you have questions about charging back, from whom are answers available?

CHARGING OUT

A. Does your library charge out?
B. For what, to whom?
C. How are charges computed? What do you feel about how the charges are computed?
D. If you have questions about charging out, from whom are answers available?

CHARGING FEES

A. What fees does your library charge, for what, and to whom?
B. How do you feel about charging fees?
C. How are charges computed? Who decides? What do you feel about how the charges are computed?
D. Does your library get to keep the fees? If not, who does?
E. If your library keeps the fees, where/how is it kept?
F. If you have questions about charging fees, from whom are answers available?

ACADEMIC LIBRARY FEE-BASED SERVICES

A. How are fee-based services managed at your academic library? Is there a separate fee-based department/service?
B. Who buys fee-based services?
C. What is sold?
D. How do other academic libraries in your area and/or comparable in size handle fee-based services?
E. How are fees collected? What happens to the money?
F. What are the annual budget and expenses?
G. How do fee-based services relate to the goals of your library?
H. If you have fee-charging questions, from whom are answers available?

PUBLIC LIBRARY FEE-BASED SERVICES

A. How are fee-based services managed at your public library? Is there a separate fee-based department/service?
B. Who buys fee-based services?
C. How do other public libraries in your area and/or comparable in size handle fee-based services?
D. How are fees collected? What happens to the money?
E. What is the budget of the fee-based service?
F. How do fee-based services relate to the goals of your library?
G. If you have fee-charging questions, from whom are answers available?

FEE-BASED SERVICES IN SPECIAL LIBRARIES

A. How are fee-based services managed at your special library?
B. Is there a separate fee-based department/service?
C. Who buys fee-based services?
D. How do other special libraries in your area handle fee-based services?
E. How do libraries elsewhere in your company handle fee-based services?
F. How are fees collected? What happens to the money?
G. What are the annual budget and expenses?
H. How do fee-based services relate to the goals of your organization?
I. If you have fee-charging questions, from whom are answers available?

WHAT TO CHARGE?

A. How are fees computed?
B. Who decides what the fees will be?
C. What do you feel about how fees are computed?
D. How do the fees relate to the goals of your organization?
E. If you have questions about what to charge, from whom are answers available?

MARKETING FEE-BASED SERVICES

A. Who does the marketing for the fee-based service?
B. How is this marketing done?

THE INDEPENDENT SECTOR

A. Does your library refer clients to independent librarians?
B. Who are the independent librarians in your area?

NOTES

1. General materials about fees for library services include William L. Whitson, "The Way I See It: Free, Fee, or Subsidy? The Future Role of Libraries," *College and Research Library News* 55:7 (July/August 1994): 427. Includes a discussion of libraries' roles of providing access, gateways, and assistance. "At most, fees might be levied for 'luxury services' such as document delivery. I believe the time has come for us to begin to provide 'differentiated access'—some resources free, others for a fee."

    For an extensive treatment of fees and information services, my *Mind Your Own Business: A Guide for the Information Entrepreneur* (New York: Neal-Schuman, 1987); *Making Money: Fees for Library Services* (New York: Neal-Schuman, 1989); "Librarians as Money Makers: The Bottom Line," *American Libraries* 21:10 (November 1990): 946–48; "Charging Back, Charging Out, Charging Fees," *Bottom Line* 4:3 (Fall 1990): 32–35; "Information Brokering: State of the Art," *Wilson Library Bulletin* 63:8 (April 1989): 55–57.

    A newsletter specific to charging library fees is *Fee for Service*, "a quarterly newsletter for libraries and information professionals offering fee-based information services" published by Whitmell & Associates, 350 Gerrard Street East, Unit 2, Toronto, Ontario, Canada M5A 2G7, tel. 416-963-9723, fax 416-963-5074. Editor Vicki Whitmell organized a Fee for Service conference in Toronto in October 1995, and plans another in 1997.

    Newsletters with frequent coverage of fee-based services are *Corporate Library Update* (bimonthly) and *Library Hotline* (weekly), published by Library Journal and written by Susan S. DiMattia, 44 Chatham Road, Stamford, CT 06903, tel. 203-322-9055, fax 203-968-9396. Both newsletters have frequent articles and news about libraries and fees.

    Directories of fee-based services include *Internet Plus Directory of Express Library Services* (American Library Association, 1997). One of the editors, Steve Coffman (who directs the fee-based service FYI at the County of Los Angeles Public Library), predicts that the *Internet Plus Directory* (which was being finalized as this book went to press) will have about 1,000 listings. *Internet Plus Directory* updates 1993's *FISCAL Directory of Fee-Based Research and Docu-*

ment Supply Services, which included 445 entries. Steve Coffman can be reached at coffman@cerf.net. Check out also *The Burwell World Directory of Information Brokers* (Houston: Burwell Enterprises), which includes fee-based services in libraries and is published approximately once a year. Burwell Enterprises' address is 3724 FM 1960 West #214, Houston, TX 77068, tel. 281-537-9051, fax 281-537-8332, e-mail 75120.50@ compuserve.com. The 1995–1996 edition contained 1,776 entries representing 51 countries. (This directory is also available on CD-ROM and on the World Wide Web at www.burwellinc.com) Burwell's newsletter, *Information Broker*, has a column called "The Library Sector" by Steve Coffman (see above) about library fee-based services.

2. Seventeen hundred hours per year really is pretty much full-time. An easy way to determine possible annual billable hours is to multiply 50 (weeks) times 40 (hours per week) to arrive at 2,000 hours. Many attorneys are expected to bill at least 1,700 hours per year.

3. Payment of overdue fines has been complicated by individual libraries' overdue rates. In a library consortium, a patron may be allowed to return books to any consortium library, no matter from where the book was borrowed. Patrons with large numbers of overdue books tend to return their books to the consortium library with the lowest overdue fees.

4. Details about this library appear in: Vicki Whitmell, "Fee-Based Profile: University of Toronto Business Information Centre," *Fee for Service* 1:4 (September 1994): 60–63. This article is based on a presentation given by Ms. Whitmell at the May 1994 meeting of the Canadian Association for Information Science.

5. An organization specific to academic libraries that charge fees is the American Library Association's FISCAL (Fee-based Information Service Centers in Academic Libraries). To join FISCAL's computer bulletin board, send an e-mail to FISC-L@listserv.nodak.edu; leave the subject line blank; as a message, write "subscribe FISC-L yourfirstname yourlastname". (To unsubscribe, the message would be "signoff FISC-L".) FISCAL makes available an informational and instructional packet called *FISCAL Primer*, available from Gelman Library Information Service (GLIS), George Washington University, 2130 4th St. NW, Room B07, Washington, DC 20052. There are two annual FISCAL *Newsletters*.

A newsletter distributed by a fee-based service in an academic library is *TechBits Newsletter*, published by Technical Information Service (TIS), Purdue University, 1206 Potter

Building room 364M, West Lafayette, IN 47907, tel. 317-494-9876, 800-289-3144 or fax 317-494-0142. In 1992, TIS carried out a study of customer satisfactions/reactions to TIS services; copies may still be available.

6. Material on public library fee-based services includes Susan Goldberg's chapter "The Entrepreneurial Library" in Linda F. Crismond, ed., *Against All Odds: Case Studies on Library Financial Management* (Atkinson, WI: Highsmith, 1993), 205–216. Crismond is the former director of the Minneapolis (Minnesota) Public Library; the article is about their fee-based service INFORM, which was established in 1970 to "provide customized in-depth reference service to clients with information needs too extensive or too specialized to be handled by other library departments on a cost-recovery basis."

7. Readings about fee-based services in special libraries include:

   - Joan Gervino, "Establishing Fees for Service," *Marketing Treasures* 8:3 (January/February 1995): 4–6. (Details on *Marketing Treasures* appear in note 10.) Discusses the Center for Banking Information at the American Bankers Association in Washington, DC.
   - The chapter "Charging Back, Charging Out, Charging Fees" in Alice Sizer Warner's *Owning Your Numbers: An Introduction to Budgeting for Special Libraries* (Washington, DC: Special Libraries Association, 1992), 63–74.
   - Leslie Clague, "Charging for Information Services: Is There a Best Way for Internal and External Cost Recoveries?" *New Zealand Libraries* 50:1 (March 1991): 12–14. The author is divisional manager of Fact Finders, a division of C. M. Research Associates, a for-profit marketing research firm whose goal is not only total cost recovery but also profit. The primary messages are: charge enough, know what you want to achieve, keep it simple, include all overheads, add a contingency factor of at least 20 percent.
   - Arthur Downing, "The Consequences of Offering Fee-Based Services in a Medical Library," *Bulletin of the Medical Library Association* 78:1 (January 1990): 57–63.
   - Alice Sizer Warner, "Special Libraries and Fees," *Special Libraries* 80:4 (Fall 1989): 275–79.

8. There is much work to be done in the broad field of outsourcing (a business concept) as applied to libraries. At

present, the author is preparing a one-day seminar on the subject of outsourcing, to be presented initially at a Special Libraries Association Conference.

9. An article on pricing is Beth Blevins, "Insider Stories: How Librarians Are Pricing Their Information Services," *Library Management Quarterly* 12:3 (Summer 1989): 10–12.

10. The two newsletters that deal with advertising and marketing are *Marketing Treasures*, edited by Chris Olson (857 Twin Harbor Drive, Arnold, MD 21012, tel. 410-647-6708, fax 410-647-0415, e-mail olson@access.digex.net); and *Marketing Library Services*, edited by Kathy Miller (143 Old Marlton Pike, Medford, NJ 08055–8750, tel. 609-654-4888, fax 609-654-4309).

11. Materials by Alice Sizer Warner about marketing and selling information services include a chapter called "Sales and Marketing" in *Mind Your Own Business*, another called "Selling" in *Making Money*.

12. For discussion of using simple language, see Anne Woodsworth's "Jettisoning the Jargon," *Library Journal* 121: 17 (15 October 1996): 41.

13. For specific suggestions on designing a brochure, see Warner, *Making Money*, pp. 122–23.

14. Burwell Enterprises, *World Directory of Information Brokers*.

15. Details about organizations of entrepreneurial librarians are:

    - ILERT (Independent Librarians Exchange Round Table) at The American Library Association, 50 E. Huron Avenue, Chicago, IL 60611, tel. 800-545-2433.
    - Consultants' Section of the Management Division of the Special Libraries Association, 1700 18th St. NW, Washington, DC 20009–2508, tel. 202-234-4700, fax 202-265-9317, e-mail sla1@capcon.net.
    - AIIP (Association of Independent Information Professionals), 234 West Delaware Avenue, Pennington, NJ 08534, tel. 609-730-8759, fax 609-730-8469, e-mail 73263.34@ compuserve.com. AIIP members can participate in a monitored, interactive listserv/bulletin board and also receive discounts from many vendors and/or suppliers. AIIP keeps up to date about local groups of information brokers and will make referrals as appropriate. Most local groups welcome non-AIIP people.

16. Two items may be of special interest to those exploring the independent sector: Sue Rugge and Alfred Glossbrenner, *The Information Broker's Handbook*, 3d ed. (New York:

McGraw-Hill, 1997); and the constantly updated *Burwell's Bibliography on Information Brokering* (Houston, TX: Burwell Enterprises), available from 3724 FM 1960W #214, Houston, TX 77068, tel. 281-537-9051, fax 281-537-8332.

7 LIVING WITH THE BUDGET

This chapter addresses ongoing budget issues and tasks, including: keeping track of the budget, planning the budget, the budget and a new job, the budget and a new library, presenting the budget, and a final section on when budget cuts loom. Whole books and many articles have been written about most of these subjects, and many are indicated for further study.

KEEPING TRACK OF THE BUDGET

The financial manager (usually the director) of any library is responsible for planning, directing, and monitoring the library's budget on a day-to-day basis as well as over the long term; no one knows more about the library's budget, no one cares more about the library's budget. This person must be completely familiar with library budget numbers and keep them up to date and under control. He or she must also constantly monitor how the library fits into the larger picture—whatever that picture is.

A library manager with long experience, both at a private research laboratory and at two leading universities, once said:

> Management is a contact sport. If you want to be in with the grownups, be in charge of your money. Make sure you have your ducks in a row when presenting a budget. Remember, people *aren't* against you in financial planning. They are merely *for themselves*. Get to know the jargon of accounting. Read what your manager reads, tie into whatever that kind of thinking is. Pick your battles, know the difference between a battle and a war. Do not mistake the edge of the rut for the horizon. How are you communicating? Is it as management wants to hear it? . . . Remember: *nobody* knows our business as we do.[1]

In most organizations, budget details are kept on a computer at headquarters. Printouts are sent to each manager, including the library manager, on a regular basis. Quickly learn how to read (i.e., how to scan and check) these printouts. As one new academic library director said, "It took me two minutes to learn how to make sense of those big, floppy printouts, and it's lucky it didn't take longer—that was all the time I had."[2]

While these printouts are important, you should not depend on them as your only mechanism for keeping track of where your budget stands. Successful library managers recommend that you keep tabs on it yourself, as well, item by item, either with a pencil or (preferably) on a spreadsheet. Virtually all guest lecturers at our library school's fiscal management classes have produced examples of how they do it, and point out that keeping track yourself often involves more detailed breakdown within budget lines than appears on the headquarters budget.

A library's director might keep track of the budget as follows:[3]

Expenditures as of [date]

Item	Budget	Spent to date	% spent	$ remaining
Personnel	_____	_____	_____	_____
Books	_____	_____	_____	_____
Software	_____	_____	_____	_____
Misc.	_____	_____	_____	_____
TOTALS	_____	_____	_____	_____

There are many reasons for keeping your own record of expenditures, the most important of which is timeliness: reporting from any organization's financial office can lag by weeks, and your library should be monitored more closely than that. Also, if you keep your own up-to-date and accurate records, errors in headquarters' records are simple to spot and easy to substantiate.

PLANNING THE BUDGET

Budget planning for any library—new, old, academic, public, special, school—is a constant process. There is no "budget time of year": all the time is budget time.[4]

Let's look at the Simmonsville Public Library[5] as an example. A recent year's budget is pictured on a simple spreadsheet in Figure 7.1.

At Simmonsville, all manner of scenarios are tried by library students. We award substantial raises to all staff, of course, and we encourage them to go to faraway meetings at library expense. We replace the furnace, we get more OPACs, we fix the leak in the roof. We anticipate that the Friends of the Library will contribute incredible amounts of money. The stock market is truly bullish, so the library's endowment fund will produce lavishly. Then we tell the Simmonsville town treasurer what we think and what we want and (presto! chango!) we miraculously get what we ask for. The Simmonsville simplistic model serves as an effective teaching tool. Unfortunately, real library life is financially—and politically—a good deal more cruel.

Veteran library directors say that the first step in planning next year's official budget is to figure out what next year's budget must be in order to be able to continue what is being done this year, and to pinpoint what increases can be expected so as to make

Figure 7.1 Simmonsville Public Library Budget					
A	**B**	**C**	**D**	**E**	**F**
1	FY99			FY00	
2 INCOME					
3 Town	80,000				
4 Endowment	5,000				
5 Other	15,000				
6 TOTAL		100,000			
7					
8 EXPENSES					
9 Personnel	70,000				
10 Materials	15,000				
11 Operations	10,000				
12 All else	5,000				
13 TOTAL		100,000			

this happen. Usually, library managers receive guidelines from their organizations within which future planning must proceed, such as "x percent maximum total budget increase" and "fringe benefits increase of x percent." For example, a general guideline for budgeting was issued to all departments (including the public library) in Foxboro, Massachusetts. There were twelve specific guidelines, some of which indicated that, were assistance needed, to contact the town accountant. One guideline required full explanation of any budget line that increased or decreased more than 10 percent and/or was more than $1,000. The guidelines also demanded details to explain any line new to or eliminated from the budget. Those twelve guidelines indicated the town's budget submission rules for that particular year; it behooved the director of the public library to follow those rules to the letter.

When planning your budget, be sure to contact those who sell to your library. Subscriptions agencies, publishers, and vendors offer guidelines on expected price increases for their industries' wares.

Be sure to ask staff to specify any increases they see and to provide "wish lists." What, ideally, do staff feel is needed to serve users better, to make staff lives easier and more productive? Get staff priorities, involve staff as much as possible, get them to help you get prices. Ask reference people about online costs, about supplies. Check into equipment maintenance, equipment rental. Gather as much information from as many sources as seem appropriate, get as much information as is possible to create a budget for next year that will keep you functioning as well as you are functioning this year.[6]

Prepare this status quo budget as a line-item budget, making the total meet all appropriate guidelines. Next, express the line-item budget as a program budget that outlines how programs are allied to the goals of the library and the goals of the parent organization. (When presenting the budget, it is prudent to have both line-item and program versions available.) Will following guidelines allow for fulfillment of goals? If you feel library service will be seriously threatened by following given guidelines, prepare an alternate line-item budget reflecting this. The consensus is that if you do not ask for money, you will never get it. Show exactly what benefits will result from your alternate, increased budget. Translate the new line-item budget into a program budget.

When doing this planning and budgeting, think carefully; "padding" a budget (i.e., asking for more than you actually need, while expecting to receive less than you ask for) is a poor idea. It is better to be realistic and believable; if necessary, explain to those who allocate your parent organization's finances that your budget request will in no way be "padded." If you sincerely feel it would benefit your organization to make substantial changes in your library's budget (adding people, creating new services), forewarn the powers that be in writing as early as possible, possibly a year or two ahead of when you foresee the increases. And do remember to keep your language jargon free.

The trick to thinking into the future is not to forget what is happening now. Many library budget managers order the bulk of their materials early in the budget year so they can pay for them during the year: the time between placing orders and paying invoices can be astonishingly long.

If materials money is not entirely spent and the end of the fiscal year is approaching, be sure to spend it. Consider increasing prepayments to deposit accounts. Subscriptions agencies may give discounts for early payment. A director of a small public library walks over to a nearby bookstore on the last day of the fiscal year to buy items ("at expensive prices," he says) on his wish list. In New England, a library bindery will actually make "house calls" to pick up advance payment checks.[7]

THE BUDGET AND A NEW JOB

Every town, every school, every college, every company, every institution is different. So a new job always means learning new budget rules, such as:

- What are the goals for the library?
- What are goals for the organization?
- Is the library part of a profit-making organization, or of a nonprofit (not-for-profit) organization?
- Who "owns" the library?
- Who holds library purse strings?
- What are the financial realities?
- What is the larger financial picture?
- What is the fiscal year?
- What is the budget cycle, the budget calendar?
- When does planning start on next year's budget?
- When are guidelines expected for that planning?
- From whom is fiscal guidance available?

Are there budget elements that have calendars of their own? Some libraries have hard-to-predict cycles for equipment, furniture, or computers. Government library budgets often do not include personnel, and personnel budgets may carry their own timing. Ask. Another timing question: will there be mid-fiscal-year changes?

How careful do you need to be to keep each budget line separate from the others? How much shifting between lines is acceptable, assuming the total budget is not exceeded? Each organization has its own rules about budget lines.

Librarians often think they must do everything alone, but there is always budget help available: the treasurer, the accounting office, the chief financial officer, the controller. Do as much as you can first, then ask for help.

THE BUDGET AND A NEW LIBRARY

Since special librarians typically cope with starting a brand new library more than once in a career, they learn quickly.[8] They seek help from budgeting gurus within their organizations. They measure, they look into cost of space, they consider timing, they hope they will find some assistance. They sort piles of files, they spot duplications, they target out-of-date materials. They find out what the organization already spends on publications, information equipment, information services; they discover what the organization already has. They ask about how people are getting information now, what people are doing now. They try to keep equipment costs separate from collection costs; they try to use effectively what the organization already owns.

Special librarians starting a new library emphasize to employers and staffers that the library is to be a conduit to information, not primarily a storehouse. And when librarians handle "donations" of books and magazines and reports, they quickly learn not to promise to keep what is donated: usually there is a lot of discarding and clarification about "collection development policies."

While all this is going on, the library and its librarian(s) must serve the organization's needs. As one special librarian said, "Well, I started with just a chair, a telephone on the floor, and a copy of the *World Almanac* that I had brought from home. By 10 A.M. that first morning I was involved in an interlibrary loan; by noon I was farming out an online search and vowing to get myself equipped before the week was out. When I came back from lunch there were piles of old magazines all over the floor." Librarians starting new libraries remember rule-of-thumb budget standards and make themselves very familiar with all aspects of their organization's financial picture.

School librarians face yet other challenges in starting new libraries. Living with a school library budget, especially in a new school, can be one of our profession's greatest challenges. The following observations were offered by veteran school librarians who advised on preparation of this book.[9] "Every school system is run as a fiefdom, you really have to know your turf," said one. According to another: "There is a huge discrepancy between what the budget says and what is actually spent—you have to watch out that other departments don't dump their costs on your budget, especially computers. And how do you decide if CD-ROMs are software or books?" A state-level librarian complained, "School reports in the various towns are impossible to compare." And the refrain: "People—salaries—don't appear on school budgets (so they are 'free'?); what about the librarian who *boasted* about spending seventeen hours on the Internet—*some*one's paying that salary!"

THE BUDGET AND A NEW BUILDING

For librarians charged with the actual building of a brand new library, serious thought should be given to having what is called a "*charrette*." Charrette (the French word for "cart") comes from a century ago, in Paris, where at the Ecole des Beaux-Arts, students were given assignments that were due at very specific times (apparently often at midnight). At the appointed hour, a cart was pushed about the room to collect the assignments; students were known literally to climb aboard the charrette as it came by, so final assignment touches could be added.

A library application of the charrette occurred in the design of a public library in Wisconsin.[10] Part of the contract with the library was that building must start no longer than nine months after the contract was signed: no time could be wasted. So a team from the architectural office came to Wisconsin for the better part of a week to participate in a charrette. Joining them were other building experts (such as a landscaper and wiring and plumbing and heating engineers), a library consultant, a model maker, a cost control expert, secretarial backup, and the like. The goal was to produce the "schematic design" (architecture's first phase) at the end of that week.

Bear in mind that much work had happened before the charrette could begin: the city had decided to build a new library and presumably knew where the money would come from; a library site had been selected, a library building statement had been prepared; architects had studied appropriate local building codes and the site itself; the city provided work space and equipment for the charrette to happen and invited appropriate local people to attend.

They began on Sunday afternoon with a tour, and on Monday there first was an informational meeting for anyone who wanted to know what was going to happen that week. As the week went on, the architects had separate meetings with the mayor's office; with the library's staff, board, director, and building committee; with the city planning, cable television, and public works departments; with the commission for the disabled—in other words, with any and all agencies that would impact on the building. Architects worked far into the evening each day, turning what had been learned into designs and sketches. Each morning, architects posted progress reports. The charrette room was open during the week and the public was invited to come in. By the last day, a forty-eight-page "brochure" had been put together with floor plans, elevations, furniture layouts, and cost estimates. The architects made their final presentation late on the last afternoon, followed by a trustees' meeting to approve this schematic design phase.

Any prudent library director or financial officer budgeting for a new library building, or for a substantial building addition, must be involved not only in how and when money is spent while construction proceeds but also and in all aspects of the physical structure as well. A librarian from New Mexico writes that "designing an architecturally advanced and technologically superior library building can often be fraught with unexpected peril. Librarians who innocently imagine that they need only worry about space utilization and traffic patterns may wish, in hindsight, that they'd been issued a hard hat."[11]

New, modern libraries have high-tech electronic and mechanical equipment that low-tech librarians and custodians are not necessarily trained for. Therefore, as budget watchdog and information specialist, the top person, the director, must procure and keep directions, manuals, and details about every aspect of the library's new building since these are virtually impossible to get other than at the time of construction and installation. Procure them, copy them, catalog them, keep them, and never lend away the last copy. Do not depend on the maintenance department to have these materials; if you do, your library may have to spend unbudgeted money in the future.

A fiscally prudent librarian will watch that new construction is not too high-tech. For instance, it is very expensive, as time goes on, to have computerized climate control in a building where windows cannot be opened: if the computer control dies, that computer may be difficult and expensive to fix fast—and while you are waiting, people may badly need fresh air. Also, buy local: it is very costly to buy replacement parts from faraway vendors who do not make house calls or installations.

PRESENTING THE BUDGET

How, where, and to whom a library budget is presented varies, of course, from library to library.[12] There are, however, a few common denominators applicable to all budget presentations.

All librarians know well how crucial it is that those who make decisions about the library's budget are those who cannot get along without the library. The motto is: "Be sure to serve those who hold the purse strings." Remember that budget planners have many budgets to review, and be brief, be to the point, be informed, speak simply.[13] Budget reviewers prefer not to be overwhelmed with paperwork, so present them only with what is essential. Visual aids help a lot. If you have circulated material ahead of time, assume no one has read what you gave them—and don't make anyone feel embarrassed or awkward if they have not done appropriate homework.[14]

Present your budget in exactly the format expected by budget reviewers: follow all guidelines. Although the format is almost always a line-item budget, remember to have a program budget with you (the same budget in program format) with line-item expenditures divided up between programs. If you are asked why a particular line is so high and it is suggested that the line be reduced, produce the program budget and ask which program or programs the budget reviewers feel should absorb the cut. This helps them focus on what the library is trying to accomplish.

Be able to justify each line on your budget. Be honest. Explain what you have suggested be cut out, what does not appear in your budget. Tell about what you do not want funds for.

In presenting the library budget, show your understanding of budget managers' priorities. Know what kind of a year your organization is having, the overall picture. Remember, though, that you know more about libraries than the budget reviewers do (you are the library expert). Be clear, be easy to understand, make it easy for budget people to agree with you.[15]

At budget presentation time it may be appropriate to produce what many of us call our "anecdotal and testimonial ammunition"—i.e., short tales of how the library gave extraordinary service, or copies of letters (and e-mails) of thanks to the library and its staff. (One special librarian was overheard to say, "Ask users how much money the company saved each time you do a search, and then throw this back at them at budget time!")

WHEN BUDGET CUTS LOOM

When you are facing budget cuts, remember that you and your library are part of a larger team: be loyal.[16] When discussing budget cuts with budget managers, express what each cut will mean to library users; explain what users will no longer have, what users will be unable to request, what users will now have to wait for. Underplay what budget cuts will mean to library staff. And involve your library staff with budget cuts. What do they suggest? How do they feel, what are their ideas?

Do not wait for budget cuts to happen; be thinking ahead, encourage your staff to think ahead. If, for instance, some program is not working, stop it. Explore improvements in buying, in processing. Explore cooperations between libraries, within your library system.

Try to look at impending budget cuts as a way to clean house. Consider ways in which the library might save money, explore ways in which the library might create income of its own. Is this the time to establish a fee-based service? Should a program be started involving volunteers? Should a capital fund drive be held? How about money raisers, book sales, fairs? Perhaps money could be saved by shortening library hours: closing on Sundays in summer, closing Friday evenings, not opening until noon.

Many suggest that the library cut out those items that people will not tolerate, that will cause most complaint (popularly known as the "bitch cut system"). Cut something that shows, that hurts. For instance, several years ago when the Library of Congress faced a cutback, they chose visibility: they closed on Saturdays. Money was miraculously found so they could reopen on this most popular day of the week. Public libraries find that items most visible and therefore most missed are museum passes, new media (videotapes, CDs), and the local paper. Special librarians agree that the cut that hurts most is desk copies of newspapers—people really like getting their own *New York Times* or *Wall Street Journal* and will loudly complain when the paper no longer appears.

LIVING WITH THE BUDGET

Budgets are always with us. We keep track of them, we plan them, we find new budget circumstances whenever we build a new library or change from one existing job to another. We present our budgets, we pray for bigger budgets, yet often we must have less money than we wish. Budgets do not go away. It behooves all librarians, no matter what their responsibilities or tasks, to show, visibly and openly, budget awareness and budget knowledge.

QUESTIONS TO HELP YOU FOCUS

KEEPING TRACK OF THE BUDGET
    A. What mechanisms are you now using to keep track of your library's budget?
    B. What spreadsheet program are you using?

PLANNING THE BUDGET
    A. What is the budget calendar for your organization?
    B. Have you received guidelines from your organization?
    C. Do some budget elements have calendars of their own?
    D. How much flexibility do you have regarding budget lines?
    E. May budget changes be made other than at annual budget time?
    F. What are "wish lists" of your staff? Can wishes be included in the budget?
    G. Prepare a line-item budget.
    H. Prepare a program budget based on the line-item budget.

THE BUDGET AND A NEW JOB
    A. Determine, in detail, what the budget rules are for your new job.
    B. Determine the current status of the library's budget. How do you feel about the current library budget?
    C. If you have budget questions in your new job, from whom are answers available?

THE BUDGET AND A NEW LIBRARY

A. Determine, as best you can, your organization's expectations for your new library's services and what the organization thinks the library will cost.
B. What does the organization already spend for informational materials? What is already available?
C. What are both the real and the perceived information needs of the organization?
D. Would conducting a planning charrette be useful?
E. Based on answers to the above questions, prepare two budgets: a one-time budget for creating the library, and a one-year budget for operating the library once it has been created.

THE BUDGET AND A NEW BUILDING

A. Seriously consider a library-planning charette.
B. Determine the timetable for building your new library: check with construction people and architect.
C. Collect, duplicate, and catalog *all* equipment manuals and directions for your new building.

PRESENTING THE BUDGET

A. To whom, where, and when do you present your library's budget?
B. Have you followed all guidelines?
C. Have you prepared a program budget as well as a line-item budget?
D. Are you aware of the larger financial picture of which your library is a part?
E. Do you have testimonials? Have you collected and can you produce evidence showing how patrons have been helped by your library?

WHEN BUDGET CUTS LOOM

A. To repeat the question immediately above, are you aware of the larger financial picture of which your library is a part?
B. What budget cuts has your library already carried out?
C. If you are asked to absorb a further budget cut, what would library users have to do without? What would they tolerate? What would they not tolerate?

NOTES

1. From a guest lecture at the Simmons Fiscal Management class by Ann Wolpert, currently director of libraries at Massachusetts Institute of Technology.
2. Remark made to the author by the late Patricia King when she assumed directorship of the Schlesinger Library at Radcliffe College in Cambridge, Massachusetts.
3. There are obviously many ways to keep track of a budget. Some libraries want to know what has been spent, for instance, in the current month. A colleague writing privately on this subject said, "We do a current month, year to date, and percent of the budget spent for each line item." Virtually every library keeps track of the budget slightly differently.
4. Among readings on planning the budget are:

   - Richard S. Rounds, *Basic Budgeting Practices for Librarians*, 2d ed. (Chicago: American Library Association, 1994). One reviewer writes: "For anyone who must plan and present a budget, this is one book which should be kept on the administrator's desk as he/she plans and implements the library budget" (*One-Person Library: A Newsletter for Librarians and Management* 11:8 [December 1994]: 5). The book includes extensive bibliographies.
   - Murray S. Martin, "The Changing Library Environment," *Library Trends* 42:3 (Winter 1994): 478–89. "There has been emerging gradually a new kind of budget model based less on the warehouse characteristics of the past and more on the consumer responsive nature of other service industries." Libraries must adapt to change while their budgets shrink, leading to greater inter-library cooperation and more library consortia.
   - Peggy Johnson, "Dollars and Sense: Real Money," *Technicalities* 10:2 (February 1990): 10–13. This article opens with a quote from former Senator Everett Dirksen, "A billion here, a billion there—pretty soon it adds up to real money." Effective budgets and budgeting processes are tools for choosing, planning and controlling activities that lead to goals.

   Readings on budget allocations include:

- Murray S. Martin, *Collection Development and Finance: A Guide to Strategic Library-Materials Budgeting* (Chicago: American Library Association, 1995).
- "Allocation Formulas for Materials Budgets," *American Libraries* 26:3 (March 1995): 225. As part of the question and answer "Action Exchange" column, a New Hampshire librarian asks others' experiences regarding allocations based on collections use.
- Mollie Niemeyer et al., "Balancing Act for Library Materials Budgets: Use of a Formula Allocation," *Technical Services Quarterly* 11:1 (1993): 43–60. Outline of allocations formula steps used over the years at Central Missouri State University's library.

5. The Simmonsville Public Library case was developed for the course LS520B ("Fiscal Management of Libraries and Information Systems") at Simmons Graduate School of Library and Information Science in Boston, Massachusetts.

6. For a discussion of next year's budget being based on a percent up (or down) from this year's (rather than on programs), see Herbert S. White, "The Tragic Cost of Being Reasonable," *Library Journal* 116:3 (15 February 1991): 166–67.

7. Other useful readings on budget planning include:

- Evan St. Lifer et al., "Public Libraries Face Fiscal Challenges," *Library Journal* 121:1 (January 1996): 40–45.
- Barbara L. Dewey, "Personnel Costs and Patterns in Libraries," *Library Trends* 42:3 (Winter 1994): 537–46. Personnel expenses should be based on priorities among library programs rather than on formulas.
- Eldred Smith and Peggy Johnson, "How to Survive the Present While Preparing for the Future: A Research Library Strategy," *College and Research Libraries* 54:5 (September 1993): 389–96. How research libraries will best survive by cooperating with each other.
- W. Patrick Leonard, "This Year Is Different: Facing Outcome Assessment," *Journal of Academic Librarianship* 18:4 (September 1992): 228ff. A dialog between a library director and the Vice Chancellor at Purdue University about the library's remaining competitive in "the contemporary budget arena."
- Robert Burgin and Patsy Hansel, "Library Management: A Dialogue: Budging the Budget," *Wilson Library Bulletin* 66:5 (January 1992): 73–75. Gives very practical advice on asking for money: be honest, don't whine, do your homework, be brief, don't get the money you re-

quested for one purpose and then spend it on something else, etc.

- Betty J. Turock and Andrea Pedolsky, *Creating a Financial Plan: A How-To-Do-It Manual for Librarians* (New York: Neal-Schuman, 1992). A workbook to help librarians match financial resources to priorities. Includes forms, worksheets, glossary.
- Jane B. Robbins and Douglas L. Zweizig, eds., *Keeping the Book$: Public Library Financial Practices* (Ft. Atkinson, WI: Highsmith, 1992).

8. Further discussion of special librarians starting a library from scratch appears in my *Owning Your Numbers*, pp. 77–78.

9. The school librarians who made these statements asked to remain anonymous.

10. For a description of how this charrette worked, see the architect's article: Edward H. Healey, "Planning a Library in One Week," *American Libraries* 22:4 (April 1991): 302–304. This article, however, deals little of how the library was going to be paid for (we can only assume appropriate money had been raised) or of how budgets were estimated as the charrette week went on. To be effective from a budget point of view, a charrette team must include a spreadsheet expert to keep close tabs on plans as they emerge.

11. Jeannette Woodward, "The Tale of the Terribly High Tech Library Building," *American Libraries* 26:4 (April 1995): 308–310. The author is at the College of Santa Fe in New Mexico, and says her writing is "a composite of the painful experiences of several librarians working in academic and public library settings, but each and every crisis did occur."

12. Look at W. Patrick Leonard, "This Year Is Different: Facing Outcome Assessment." *Journal of Academic Librarianship* 18:4 (September 1992):228+.

13. For specific suggestions on using strong, simple language, see Richard Lederer's "Strength of a Single Syllable" (taken from his book *The Miracle of Language*), *Reader's Digest* 138:830 (June 1991): 157–58.

14. Chris Bradley, "Notes From the Far Side: Town Council Budget Sessions Viewed by One Librarian," *Library Journal* 115: 17 (15 October 1990): 58.

15. Two articles about presenting budgets might be useful. The first is about a California community in danger of losing a branch library under construction; they were able to convince property owners that their property would increase in value if the library stayed: Jeffrey M. Cooper and Marilyn

C. Crouch, "Benefit Assessment Helps Open Doors," *American Libraries* 25:3 (March 1994): 232–34. The second article is Barbara Spiegelman and Kemberly A. Meiners, "13 Ideas to Transform Your Library—and the Way Management Perceives it," *SpeciaList* 17:10 (October 1994): 1ff. About how to be on the cutting edge of change, how to be the first to suggest change, or to adapt to changing circumstances—so the library is essential to the organization.

16. About budget cuts, see my "Money Matters: Six Hints for Information Managers," *Online* 15:2 (March 1991): 26–28; and "Surviving the Recession: What's Happening Out There?" *Online* 15:13 (May 1991): 6–7.

   For specific suggestions on special libraries facing budget cuts, see my *Owning Your Numbers*, pp. 81–82.

   Other materials on the subject of decreasing budgets are:

   - Leslie Farmer, *When Your Library Budget Is Almost Zero* (Englewood, CO: Libraries Unlimited, 1993).
   - Joanne R. Euster, "Take Charge of the Future Now," *College & Research Library News* 54:2 (February 1993): 89–90. It would "be a mistake to allow ourselves to become immobilized by fiscal adversity." Makes five specific suggestions.
   - A. J. Anderson, "Why Isn't the Public Library an Essential Service?" *Library Journal* 117:4 (1 March 1992): 62–64. About a public library forced to cut 40 percent from its budget.
   - Patricia Glass Schuman and John Berry, "Tough Times Bring Tough Questions," *Library Journal* 116:18 (1 November 1991): 52–55.
   - David W. Lewis, "Eight Truths for Middle Managers in Lean Times: A Library Survivor Offers up Guidelines for Others to Follow," *Library Journal* 116:14 (1 September 1991): 157–58.
   - John N. Berry, "'Sound Bites' for Budget Fights," *Library Journal* 116:12 (July 1991): 6 [editorial].

APPENDIX: SELECTED NEWSLETTERS, BOOKS & ARTICLES ABOUT BUDGETING

NEWSLETTERS

DiMattia, Susan, ed. *Corporate Library Update*. Library Journal, 245 W. 17th St., New York, NY 10011.

————. *Library Hotline*. Library Journal, 245 W. 17th St., New York, NY 10011.

Harmon, Charles, ed. *The Bottom Line: Managing Library Finances*. MCB University Press Limited, 60/62 Toller Lane, Bradford, West Yorkshire, England BD8 9BY.

Miller, Kathy, ed. *Marketing Library Services*. Information Today Inc., 143 Old Marlton Pike, Medford NJ 08055.

Olson, Chris, ed. *Marketing Treasures*. Chris Olson & Associates, 857 Twin Harbor Drive, Arnold MD 21012.

Whitmell, Vicki, ed. *Fee for Service*. Whitmell & Associates, 350 Gerrard Street East, Unit 2, Toronto, Ontario, Canada M5A 2G7.

BOOKS

American Library Association (ALA), 50 E. Huron Avenue, Chicago IL 60611, 800–545–2433. Inquire regarding current publications.

Annual Register of Grant Support: A Directory of Funding Sources. New York: R.R. Bowker Co.

Auld, Lawrence W.S. *Computer Spreadsheets for Library Applications*. 2nd ed. Phoenix AZ: Oryx Press, 1993.

Barber, Peggy and Linda Crow. *Getting Your Grant: A How-To-Do-It Manual for Librarians*. New York: Neal-Schuman Publishers, 1992.

Burwell World Directory of Information Brokers [annual]. Houston TX: Burwell Enterprises, 3724 FM 1960 West #214, Houston TX 77068 USA.

Campbell, Katherine Noyes and Susan J. Ellis. *The (Help) I-Don't-Have-Enough-Time Guide to Volunteer Management*. Philadelphia: Energize, 1995.

Crismond, Linda F. ed. *Against All Odds: Case Studies on Library Financial Management*. Fort Atkinson WI: Highsmith Press, 1993.

Daubert, Madeline J. *Money Talk: Accounting Fundamentals for Special Librarians*. Washington DC: Special Libraries Association, 1995.

Farmer, Leslie. *When Your Library Budget is Almost Zero*. Englewood CO: Libraries Unlimited, 1993.

Flanagen, Joan. *Successful Fundraising: A Complete Handbook for Volunteers and Professionals*. Chicago: Contemporary Books Inc., May 1991.

Foundation Center, 79 5th Avenue, New York NY 10003, 212–620–4230 or 800–424–9836. Inquire regarding current publications.

Generic Volunteer Orientation Manual: Your Guide to Developing an Orientation Manual for Volunteers. Issued by the Albany OR Volunteer Support Project, 1995.

Internet Plus Directory of Express Library Services. Chicago: American Library Association, 1997.

Levin, Lillian. *Planning Library Friends' Book Sales*. Available for $10 from Middletown Library Service Center, 786 Main St., Middletown CT 06457. Checks should be payable to Friends of Connecticut Libraries.

Martin, Murray S. *Academic Library Budgets*. Greenwich CT: JAI Publishers Inc., 1993.

———. *Collection Development and Finance: A Guide to Strategic Library-Materials Budgeting*. Chicago: American Library Association, 1995.

McCune, Bonnie and Charleszine "Terry" Nelson. *Recruiting and Managing Volunteers in Libraries: A How-To-Do-It-Manual*. New York: Neal-Schuman Publishers, 1995.

Morris, Betty, John T. Gillespie & Diana L. Spirt. *Administering the School Library Media Center*. 3rd ed. New York: Bowker Publishing Co., 1992.

Neal-Schuman Publishers, 100 Varick St., New York NY 10013, 212–925–8650. Inquire regarding current publications.

Oryx Press, 4041 N. Central Ave. #700, Phoenix AZ 85012, 602–265–2631. Inquire regarding current publications.

Prentice, Ann E. *Financial Planning for Libraries*. 2nd ed. Metuchen NJ: Scarecrow Press, 1996.

Reed, Sally Gardner. *Library Volunteers—Worth the Effort! A Program Manager's Guide*. Jefferson NC: McFarland & Co., 1994.

Robbins, Jane B. and Douglas L. Zweizig, eds. *Keeping the Book$: Public Library Financial Practices*. Ft. Atkinson WI: Highsmith Press, 1992.

Rounds, Richard S. *Budgeting Practices for Librarians*. 2nd ed. Chicago: American Library Association, 1994.

Rugge, Sue and Alfred Glossbrenner. *The Information Broker's Handbook*. 3rd ed. New York: McGraw-Hill Inc., 1995.

Smith, Mark. *Collecting and Using Public Library Statistics: A How-To-Do-It Manual for Librarians*. New York: Neal-Schuman Publishers, 1996.

Special Libraries Association (SLA), 1700 18th St. NW, Washington DC 20009, 202–234–4700. Inquire regarding current publications.

Stueart, Robert D. and Barbara B. Moran. *Library Management*. 4th ed. Englewood CO: Libraries Unlimited, 1993.

Turock, Betty J. & Andrea Pedolsky. *Creating a Financial Plan: A How-To-Do-It Manual for Librarians*. New York: Neal-Schuman Publishers, 1992.

Warner, Alice Sizer. *Making Money: Fees for Library Services*. New York: Neal-Schuman Publishers, 1989.

_____. *Mind Your Own Business: A Guide for the Information Entrepreneur*. New York: Neal-Schuman Publishers, 1987.

_____. *Owning Your Numbers: An Introduction to Budgeting for Special Libraries*. Washington DC: Special Libraries Association, 1992.

_____. *Volunteers in Libraries II*. New York: R.R.Bowker Company, 1983.

ARTICLES

"Allocation Formulas for Materials Budgets." *American Libraries* 26:3 (March 1995):225.

Anderson, A.J. "Why Isn't the Public Library an Essential Service?" *Library Journal* 117:4 (1 March 1992):62–64.

Barnes, Marilyn E. "Quick and Clean: A Fast Path to Library Spreadsheet Systems." *The Bottom Line* 8:1 (Summer 1994):38–49.

Berry, John. "A Good Deal for Both." *Library Journal* 120:20 (December 1995):6.

_____. "'Sound Bites' for Budget Fights." *Library Journal* 116:12 (July 1991):6.

Blevins, Beth. "Insider Stories: How Librarians Are Pricing Their

Information Services." *Library Management Quarterly* 12:3 (Summer 1989):10–12.

Bradley, Chris. "Notes From the Far Side: Town Council Budget Sessions Viewed by One Librarian." *Library Journal* 115:17 (15 October 1990):58.

Burgin, Robert and Patsy Hansel. "Library Management: A Dialogue: Budging the Budget." *Wilson Library Bulletin* 66:5 (January 1992):73–75.

Campbell, Jerry D. "Getting Comfortable With Change: A New Budget Model for Libraries in Transition." *Library Trends* 42:3 (Winter 1994): 448–459.

Chadbourne, Robert. "Volunteers in the Library: Both Sides Must Give in Order to Get." *Wilson Library Bulletin* 67:6 (June 1993):26–27.

Clague, Leslie. "Charging for Information Services: Is There a Best Way for Internal and External Cost Recoveries?" *New Zealand Libraries* 50:1 (March 1991):12–14.

Cooper, Jeffrey M. and Marilyn C. Crouch. "Benefit Assessment Helps Open Doors." *American Libraries* 25:3 (March 1994):232–234.

"Criminal Gain." *American Libraries* 27:8 (September 1996):25.

Dewey, Barbara L. "Personnel Costs and Patterns in Libraries." *Library Trends* 42:3 (Winter 1994):537–546.

Diedrichs, Carol Pitts. "Off to See the Wizard—Demystifying Your Financial Relationships." *Library Administration and Management* 10:2 (Spring 1996):105–109.

Downing, Arthur. "The Consequences of Offering Fee-Based Services in a Medical Library." *Bulletin of the Medical Library Association* 78:1 (January 1990):57–63.

Euster, Joanne R. "Take Charge of the Future Now." *College & Research Library News* 54:2 (February 1993): 89–90.

"Funding Focus." *American Libraries* 26:11 (December 1995):1101.

Gale Research Inc. "Private Funding—An Alternative." *Library Journal* 120:6 (1 April 1995):43.

Gervino, Joan. "Establishing Fees for Service." *Marketing Treasures* 8:3 (January/February 1995):4–6.

Hall, Alan. "Budget Preparation." In Bill Katz ed., *The How-to-do-it Manual for Small Libraries* (New York: Neal-Schuman Publishers, 1988): 84–90.

Healey, Edward H. "Planning a Library in One Week." *American Libraries* 22:4 (April 1991):302–304.

Heezen, Ronald R. "Take Money for Granted: Grant Proposals That Work." *Library Journal* 116:18 (1 November 1991):62–63.

Hodolfski, Carol. "Zero-Based Budgeting: A Tool for Cutting Back." *The Bottom Line* 5:2 (Summer 1991):13–19.

Johnson, Peggy. "Dollars and Sense: Real Money." *Technicalities* 10:2 (February 1990):10–13.

Kniffel, Leonard. "Corporate Sponsorship: The New Direction in Fundraising." *American Libraries* 26:10 (November 1995):1023–1026.

Krull, Jeffrey. "Private Dollar$ for Public Libraries." *Library Journal* 116:1 (1 January 1991):65–68.

Lapsley, Andrea. "Writing Winning Grant Proposals." *The Bottom Line* 8:4 (1995):38–41.

Lederer, Richard. "Strength of a Single Syllable." *Reader's Digest* 138:830 (June 1991):157–158.

Leonard, W. Patrick. "This Year Is Different: Facing Outcome Assessment." *Journal of Academic Librarianship* 18:4 (September 1992):228+.

Lewis, David W. "Eight Truths for Middle Managers in Lean Times: A Library Survivor Offers up Guidelines for Others to Follow." *Library Journal* 116:14 (1 September 1991):157–158.

Martin, Murray S. "The Changing Library Environment." *Library Trends* 42:3 (Winter 1994):478–489.

_____. "Gifts, Grants, and Libraries." *The Bottom Line* 8:2 (1995):37–39.

McCune, Bonnie F. "The New Volunteerism: Making It Pay Off for Your Library." *American Libraries* 24:9 (October 1993):822+.

Miller, Kathy. "No-Hassle Ways to Make More Money for your Library." *MLS* 7:5&6 (1994):7–8.

Miller, Marilyn L. and Marilyn L. Shontz. "The Search for the School Library Dollar." *School Library Journal* 41:10 (1 October 1995):22–23.

Molholt, Pat. "Grantsmanship." *Information Outlook* 1:5 (May 1997):13–14.

Neal, James G. and Lynn Smith. "Responsibility Center Management and the University Library." *The Bottom Line: Managing Library Finances* 8:4 (1995):17–20.

Niemeyer, Mollie et al. "Balancing Act for Library Materials Budgets: Use of a Formula Allocation." *Technical Services Quarterly* 11:1 (1993):43–60.

Pratt, Allan D. and Ellen Altman. "Live by the Numbers, Die by the Numbers." *Library Journal* 122:7 (15 April 1997):48–49.

Rawlinson, Nora. "More parsley on the potatoes; not the potatoes." *Library Journal* 116:1 (1 January 1991):67.

Robinson, Barbara M. "Costing Question Handling and ILL/photocopying: A Study of Two State Contract Libraries." *The Bottom Line* 4:2 (Summer 1990):20–25.

Schuman, Patricia Glass and John Berry. "Tough Times Bring Tough Questions." *Library Journal* 116:18 (1 November 1991):52–55.

Sizer, Theodore R. "Rethinking 'Standards." Available for $1.00 from Coalition of Essential Schools, Box 1969, Brown University, Providence RI 02903.

Solomon, Gwen. "Where & How to Get Grants." *Electronic Learning* 10:1 (January 1991):16–19.

Spiegelman, Barbara and Kemberly A. Meiners. "13 Ideas to Transform Your Library—and the Way Management Perceives It." *SpeciaList* 17:10 (October 1994):1+.

St. Lifer, Evan et al. "Public Libraries Face Fiscal Challenges." *Library Journal* 121:1 (January 1996):40–45.

Taylor, Kimberly. "Getting to Yes: A Fundraising Attitude That Works." *The Bottom Line* 5:4 (Winter 1991–1992):32–34.

"This Is How We Did It." *The U*N*A*B*A*S*H*E*D Librarian* 19 (March 1976):3.

Warner, Alice Sizer. "Charging Back, Charging Out, Charging Fees." *The Bottom Line* 4:3 (Fall 1990):32–35.

_____. "Money Matters: Six Hints for Information Managers." *Online* 15:2 (March 1991):26–28.

_____. "Librarians as Money Makers: The Bottom Line." *American Libraries* 21:10 (November 1990):946–948.

_____. "Information Brokering: State of the Art." *Wilson Library Bulletin* 63:8 (April 1989):55–57.

_____. "Special Libraries and Fees." *Special Libraries* 80:4 (Fall 1989):275–279.

_____. "Surviving the Recession: What's Happening Out There?." *Online* 15:13 (May 1991):6–7.

Warner, Penny and Tom. "Whodunit?." *School Library Journal* 37:12 (December 1991):50.

White, Herbert S. "The Tragic Cost of Being Reasonable." *Library Journal* 116:3 (15 February 1991):166–167.

Whitmell, Vicki. "Fee-based profile: University of Toronto Business Information Centre." *Fee for Service* 1:4 (September 1994):60–63.

Whitson, William L. "The Way I See It: Free, Fee, or Subsidy? The Future Role of Libraries." *College & Research Library News* 55:7 (July/August 1994):427.

Woodsworth, Anne. "Jettisoning the Jargon," *Library Journal* 121:17 (15 October 1996):41.

Woodward, Jeannette. "The Tale of the Terribly High Tech Library Building." *American Libraries* 26:4 (April 1995):308–310.

INDEX

ABOUT THE AUTHOR

Alice Sizer Warner holds an undergraduate degree from Harvard/Radcliffe. Her MLS is from Simmons Graduate School of Library and Information Science. She is an information entrepreneur with her own firm (The Information Guild) in Lexington, Massachusetts.

She regularly teaches a course, "Fiscal Management of Libraries and Information Systems," at Simmons as well as a one-day class for the Special Libraries Association. The latter began as a class on budgeting and now is called "Mainstreaming the Library." She has also taught about library budgeting at the University of Michigan and the University of North Carolina.

Her previous books include: *Volunteers in Libraries* (R.R. Bowker Co., 1983), *Mind Your Own Business: A Guide for the Information Entrepreneur* (Neal-Schuman Publishers, 1987), *Making Money: Fees for Library Services* (Neal-Schuman Publishers, 1989), *Owning Your Numbers: An Introduction to Budgeting for Special Libraries* (Special Libraries Association, 1992), and a memoir called *Bethany* (privately printed, 1995).